Over Your Dead Body

The History and Future
of
How We Deal With the Dead

Over Your Dead Body

The History and Future of How We Deal With the Dead

Robert Connolly

Over Your Dead Body
The History and Future of How We Deal With the Dead

Copyright © Robert Connolly
October, 2015

All rights reserved. No part of this book may be reproduced in any form without the express written permission of the publisher, except by a reviewer.

Printed in the USA
First Printing in 2015

ISBN 10: 1517763630
ISBN 13: 978-1517763633

Cover Design by Robert Connolly,
with thanks to Øyvind Rauset

Contents

Introduction	1
I. A Day in the Life *Everyday tales of funeral folk*	3
II. History of Embalming *From the pharaohs to the future*	19
III. Tales from the Crypt *A diversionary tale of hair growth and casket fashions*	36
IV. British Eccentricity, Yankee Ingenuity *How embalming became popular*	43
V. Down to Earth *Why embalm? Premature burial, modern grave goods*	59
VI. Secrets of Embalming *Initiation rituals, regulation, take-overs*	67
VII. More 'Inconvenient Biochemistry' *Science of death, consequences for the undertaker*	81
VIII. Back to Balmer's… *Black bags, hearses, campness, perks of the job*	87
IX. PMs Question Time *Autopsy procedure, revelation*	95
X. Sex & Death and Art & Law *Necrophilia, body snatching today*	103

XI. Underworld Undertakers	
Crime and undertaking, trade trinkets	112
XII. The History of Undertaking	
1087-now. Kings, commoners, crape,	
jet, plumes	128
XIII. The Future of Undertaking	
Cremation, its replacements,	
ecology of death	179
Bibliography	215
About the Author	219

Introduction

20 years ago I worked for a funeral firm in a big city. I always said I'd write a book about it, that the first sentence would be *"You always know it's a bad one when the copper's stood outside."* and that the title would be "Confessions off an Undertaker".

The memories of events that I include are those that have stayed with me; they are even now still extremely vivid, distilled from my experiences by the passage of time and retained in all their immediacy in pin-sharp recall. They are all in various ways remarkable by normal standards of existence, but not at all strange in the world they are part of.

But this has turned out to be much more than a collection of stories about undertaking.

The firm I worked for no longer exists (but I have changed the names to protect the innocent – and the guilty – nonetheless), and as I interviewed people working in the trade now to check the details, somehow that process spread to include Europe, and then America and Australia.

As interesting facts discovered along the way led to other interesting facts, and brief digressions became whole sections, this has expanded from a personal account of what undertakers do, to include their history, and how they came to take over something we used to do for ourselves, the science and ecology of death today, and the future of how we deal with the dead.

I've written it so that it works as something you read from start to finish, but also as something you can dip in and out of wherever you like.

I

A Day in the Life

You always know it's a bad one when the copper's stood outside (instead of sat inside having a read of The Sun).

It was a flat above a shop, with very steep stairs right behind the front door, and the flies started as soon as you got in. Upstairs they were so bad that they were crawling up your nose and in your mouth. The smell was atrocious, the kind that gets in your hair and clothes, and that you can't wash off.

The room was knee-deep in empty beercans, so it was difficult to get through the door, and the cloud of flies was so dense it was difficult to see across the room. Somewhere in there was what the technician at St Dunstan's called a jolly green giant.

I won't go into the details of getting it out – we had to use a shell instead of the stretcher. It made you think, though. It was a woman, probably middle-aged from the amount of flesh on her (old people are, as you may have noticed yourself, usually skinny; handy in this line of business). You can't tell from the clothes – counterfeit designer sports gear is a uniform that transcends age among the drinking classes in that part of town.

Had she got a final stock of booze in, put it to hand, and buried herself in a drift of White Diamond as she drank herself to death? Or was this some kind of interior decoration quirk? I've noticed teenagers like to blu-tack cans or beermats to their walls, girls as well as boys, these days.

Jobs like that stand out, of course, but really they're all extraordinary, because working in the funeral business, you're involved in something that no-one knows about and no-one talks about.

Death is, as they say, the last taboo – but the endlessly repeated corollary to that endlessly repeated cliché, that death is for us what sex was to the Victorians, is not quite true.

Everyone, even Victorians, thinks about sex, and most have personal experience of it on a regular basis, but death now really is kept out of sight and, if not out of mind, as much as possible physically separated from life.

It seems ironic now, but I took the job because I thought I'd get funny stories out of it. A friend of mine had worked as an embalmer when he was a medical student, and according to him it was one long round of pranks and practical jokes from day one:

Two bearers eyeing a body and a coffin, shaking their heads and saying repeatedly to a new recruit

"'E won't go in there, oh no, ... E'll never go in there ...",

then, finally,

"SO WE'LL 'AVE TO PUT 'IM IN!"

They told me at the Job Centre that they didn't get many adverts from undertakers, and that this one specified previous experience essential.

That was a load of bollocks, and I could have spared myself the effort of inventing a past as a casual bearer in another time and another place, because after they'd hired me it dawned on them that everyone else there was a midget compared to me (I'm six foot one). Which made the bearing very undignified, not to say precarious, my shoulder being about eight inches higher than the other three under the coffin.

You'd think they might have thought of that beforehand. Anyway, after that they got in a young lad who didn't even pretend to any previous, who turned out to be what I can only describe as a ghoul.

Tim was a gangling streak of piss with prominent knobbly joints and a prominent knobbly adam's apple and a bad haircut. I suspect he may have even have been ESN, and I certainly had plenty of time to investigate that suspicion, because of course they paired him up with me.

It didn't help with the bearing, though. What happened was that the coffin took a pronounced foot-down attitude (the head is always at the back) and almost the entire weight was thrown onto the two at the front, which didn't make me and Tim very popular, however much we pointed out it wasn't our fault.

Having us at the front was out of the question. Experiment proved that aside from looking even more absurd, the centre of gravity being nearer the back meant that the coffin slid in that direction uncontrollably as soon as we set off.

We were forced to adopt a peculiar gliding walk with our knees bent and our backs crouched. This, coupled with the fact that professional bearers walk with hands clasped in front (not gripping the other side of the coffin, except going up or down steps, at least at funerals), made us look like Uriah Heep in stereo.

On his first day I was called into the boss's office, introduced to the lad, and was told they'd hired him because he was the same height as me.

> "And you'll be taking him out and showing him the ropes."

I'd only been there a month or two, and I was passing on the torch of knowledge as it had been passed to me, like a baton in a relay race. A torch that was burning dimly, my instructor having had no great enthusiasm for the job, and me even less.

I was down to drive the van all day, so no funerals, just shuttling bodies to and fro, from shops to and from embalming. Which might be why I'd been landed with him – you don't want someone who's never done the job before on a funeral straight off.

I waited while he was given a second-hand polyester suit that didn't fit, a mac whose sleeves were three inches too short, and a pair of black leather gloves from the wardrobes in what was obviously once a bedroom, presumably when this was the family home above the shop.

Hand in glove in glove

Tim liked the gloves. When we were sat in the van later, him proudly stroking the sleeves of his uniform as if it was from Savile Row, I watched as he took some disposable latex gloves from the box on top of the dashboard and then put them on over the leather ones that he was already wearing, so that his hands looked like packets of cling-wrapped dates.

I looked at him, baffled, while he grinned shyly.

"What have you done that for?"

"I dunno. It feels good."

We had just collected a body from the downstairs back room and put it on the van (for some reason bodies are always put 'on' the van, not 'in'). I got the impression he was fulfilling a long-held ambition when he first handled a body. It was, predictably, someone's grandad, the funeral business's number one customer. Men are supposed to die before their wives because they're worn out by a life of work and stress. I think it's just genetic – men's bodies wear out quicker. I bet that man's wife had just as hard a (pre-welfare state working class) life as he did.

Tim had had an almost touching look of childlike wonder on his face as he prodded the body's flesh and manipulated its hands.

"It's not what I thought at all. It's all soft and floppy like a big white rubber doll."

A big cold white rubber doll. At least this one was dressed and ready to go. On my first day I had been sent into the same downstairs back room with a big carrier bag full of clothes that I'd been told to put on someone's grandad.

I was quite sure that this was the first of that endless round of pranks and practical jokes that I was expecting. After all, I'd read 'The Loved One' and 'The American Way of Death', so I knew they had special shirts and suits that had a slit up the back for dressing corpses in their coffins.

My new oppo, Dave, tasked with showing me the ropes, in the same way that I would be with Tim, leaned against the wall smoking a roll-up and looking out of the window. I looked in the bag. Everything was in there, all neatly folded: shoes & socks, a three-piece suit, shirt & tie, even singlet & Y-fronts and, on top of the pile, a hankie. He won't be wiping his nose where he's going, I thought.

"Is this an open–coffin job, then?" I said, trying to go along with the joke.

Dave shrugged and stared at a bit of tobacco he'd just picked off his lip. After a bit of waiting for him to laugh and say "Gotcha!", I tried again.

"But this is a joke isn't it? I don't really have to dress him up in this lot do I? Who's going to see it?"

Dave shrugged again and said nothing. At that point Maurice, the head of the firm, who'd just given me the bag upstairs in his office, stuck his head round the door. He'd obviously been listening.

"Something wrong, Bob?"

I wasn't sure how to play this – if it was a joke, then the boss was in on it.

"Do you really want me to put these clothes on him? Aren't there special suits for this that fasten up the back?"

But Maurice obviously hadn't read Evelyn Waugh or Jessica Mitford.

"This is someone's grandad, Bob. The family have given us these clothes because they want him to be buried in them."

"So do I cut them up the back to get them on?"

Maurice frowned, and looked at me as if he wasn't sure if I was trying to wind him up.

"No. They want him to be wearing these clothes, so that's what he'll be wearing, not a load of rags."

I realised it wasn't a good idea to point out that unless they opened the coffin and took him out to look round the back, there was no way they could know.

"Ah, I see. Right, okay then."

Maurice gave me a long hard look, then left. I heard him go back upstairs, and realised I hadn't heard him come down. I got the impression I hadn't done myself too many favours there.

Grandad was wearing a shirt, cardie, polyester slacks and slippers. Getting those off was hard enough, and Dave made no move to help.

Although this was very obviously the body of an old man in his late 70s with grey hair and a moustache, fit-looking, in an ex-army kind of way, I found I was unable to rid myself of the impression that it was a cunningly-made lifesize wooden doll covered in silicone, or, yes, rubber.

I couldn't help wondering what kind of job I'd got myself into while I was trying to wrestle the pair of newly-laundered Y-fronts over his wedding tackle. The shoes were surprisingly difficult, too, because his ankles were so floppy, until I stopped trying to hold his ankle and worked out that I had to cup his heel in one hand and cram the shoe on with the other.

I realised I'd been trying to use the same technique that you would with a child, who, however unhelpful, has ankles that don't wobble all over the place.

Which gave me a marketing idea for Clarks. You remember Start Rite shoes for toddlers? Well, they could look after the other end of the market with End Rite – biodegradable and inflammable, with velcro up the back of the heel to get them on, and a clip for morgue toetags.

I was never asked to dress a body again, nor did I hear of any of the other chauffeur bearers being asked to do it. It was normally done, I think, by the embalmers, who also did the make-up.

Which, to return to new boy Tim's first day, is where we were taking someone's grandad while Tim was inventing glove puppet prophylaxis.

Black Van Man

This is what the day consisted of when you were on the van – yes, 'on' the van again, not 'driving the van'. And you, or the police, or the doctor, are always 'on way', never 'on *the* way' or 'here soon'.

Anyway, when you were on the van, you spent the day making short journeys collecting and delivering, pretty much like all the other van drivers, except your van is black or dark grey, not white. The other tell-tale signs for spotting an undertaker's van were a spinning ventilator on the roof and a driver in a white shirt & black tie. There also seems to be an increasing tendency to mark the van as an ambulance, which I suppose gets round the problem of parking tickets.

Bodies have to go from their first resting place – hospital, old people's home, their own home, pavement or wherever – to the undertaker's shop nearest the family home. Then, if the family agrees to it, they get embalmed (which involves another trip to & from the shop that has the embalming suite, unless that's where they happen to be already), dressed, and put in a coffin for the family to visit at the shop, or less usually these days, for a wake at the family home or for a vigil in church.

Larger undertakers have a head office, known by the name of the road it's in, a garage where the hearses, funeral cars and vans are kept, and subsidiary shops, one of which will be where the embalming is done. The other shops retain the names of the family businesses that used to run them, and the name plates behind the glass in the sides of the hearses are swopped over accordingly for funerals, like false number plates on James Bond's car. This gives the illusion that people are dealing with the same family business that their family has always been served by.

Old Thanatocracy

Even with this ringing, the firm we worked for, Balmer's, were still a family business, even if they only had their own name over the door at the head office at Paradise Road. Maurice was the boss, just like his dad before him, and other members of the family worked there in other capacities. Most undertakers in Britain are still independents, and often, like Balmer's, originally family businesses, who had, over time, bought up their local competitors. Genuine single shop family firms survive in larger numbers in country towns and villages.

Balmer's garage was a courtyard that had been roofed over, with a couple of small rooms leading off. I suppose these had been feed and tack rooms originally – you could see the marks on the other walls where the horse stalls had been when this was still stables.

Apart from the brief bursts of activity at the start and end of the working day when the cars left and arrived, with the engine noise and exhaust fumes book-ended by the squeal and rattle of the ceiling-high sliding entrance doors, the garage was a peaceful and contemplative place. This was due in equal parts to the chapel-like acoustics created by the high part-glazed roof, and to the sepulchral light like that of a winter's day which filtered through the peeling white-wash covering the rafters and glass panels – which also contributed a suitably snowy (or dandruff-like) effect as it fell.

One of the ceilingless rooms had a sink, a kettle, and a two-ring Baby Belling electric cooker, and I spent what seemed like a considerable amount of time on my own in there to start with, savouring the cool echoing silence and soft shadowless light, "learning routes" from the battered hardback A to Z on the table under the shelf with the teabags and sugar by the sink.

Apart from the graphics on the teabag carton and possibly the date on a discarded Sun or Star, there was nothing to peg the space to any particular era from the past 60 years. Take away the Belling and swop the stainless steel sink for ceramic, and the 60w bulb for gas, and it could have been any time from the 1880s onwards.

A persistent whiff of Victoriana often surrounds the appurtenances and procedures of undertaking.

Take the traditional window display. The look is Victorian High Church Gothic with fumed oak, stained glass and polished brass, or the more austere Arts & Crafts look with blonde oak and bright metal fittings. Traditional contents include cinerary urns, flower holders for graves, and photos of horse-drawn hearses. And when this is replaced by dried flower arrangements flanked by corporate slogans and logos, in a cack-handed attempt to make the front office look like an estate agent's, the changes usually stop at the STAFF ONLY signs.

(The best window display I ever heard of was the Co-op's in Blackburn. It was a tropical fish tank with lumps of coal sitting on crushed coal on the bottom, with black fish and a purple light at the back.)

Other modernising efforts will also be limited to what meets the public gaze – shiny grey two-piece suits instead of black jackets & waistcoats with grey pinstripe trousers, and a Volvo or Mercedes hearse instead of a Daimler.

The hearse at Balmer's was a 10 year old Ford, as were the cars. The van was clapped-out, and a bastard to drive, with a stiff clutch that had very long travel, and lots of play in the steering. Both revealed a slightly surprising capacity for corpses on opening the back door for the first time. Hearses, like double-decker buses, have 'room for one upstairs', with hidden space underneath for two more, and undertakers' vans also have 'plenty of room inside', with racks for four. Shortly after I started at Balmer's, I certainly helped the passengers move along the bus and make room for others.

Highway Hokey Cokey

It happened like this. As I said, the van was clapped out, one aspect of that being the dodgy lock on the back doors. The first time I drove it, Dave had told me it wasn't enough to turn the handle from vertical to horizontal after closing the doors, you had to actually lock it with the key. I assumed this to be just a security measure, but found out I assumed wrong when taking a roundabout at speed. I heard a noise from the back which I took to be the stretchers rattling. Then Dave glanced over his shoulder and said

"Don't look back, just brake hard!"

I did both of course, glancing in the rear view mirror to see someone's grandad and grandma hurtle back into the van on their trolleys after hanging halfway out, and the doors bang shut after them. Grandma in her nightie and slippers, grandad in cardie and Alf Garnett bags. I made bloody sure that Tim knew how dodgy the lock was when I showed him over the van on his first day.

In the past, shells were used more – rounded mummy-shaped lightweight plastic coffins – but most places now use ambulance-type stretchers with three quick-release restraining straps like car seatbelts. The posh type have an undercarriage that folds up when you bang the front legs against the van tailboard. They're called 'gurneys' in America.

Balmer's were the lightweight type, with six-inch stub legs that folded out manually, and a dark blue plastic-backed needlecord cover that fitted over the bodies and was held in place by elastic loops at the sides. If it was a messy one, a piece of clear PVC from off a roll went on the stretcher first and was folded over the body before the straps and the cover went on. Despite what you see on the telly; no body bags, except in the most exceptional circumstances, where because of the state of the body, it was best to roll or shovel it sideways into a bag. Usually, sloppy ones went into a shell, which of course someone (usually me as most junior, until Tim arrived) had to swill out afterwards. Not a nice job.

I drew Tim's attention to the little foibles of Balmer's van on our way to the shop where the embalming was done. When we arrived at Thrale's (the name of the family who originally had it, and whose name was still over the door), we took the body off the van and carried it into the shop – yes, through the same shop that customers sat in to arrange their relatives' funerals. The bereaved made their arrangements in a room separated from the front-door lobby by a door with a frosted glass window. You might expect that there'd be a service entrance, as there would be for most businesses that had a regular throughput of goods, but again you have to remember that in Britain this is a trade that has for the most part developed from Victorian beginnings by piecemeal acquisition, often in densely built-up, speculatively-developed areas.

I introduced Tim to the manager, John, who told us to put the body in the other room in the back, because the embalming room was full. John was short and skinny, in his 30s, with thinning blond hair in a side parting, watery blue eyes and bad acne scars on his cheeks that looked worse because his face always looked red raw, as if he tried to shave them off every day.

He favoured the shirt-sleeves-and-waistcoat look when he wasn't seeing to customers, like a saloon card dealer in a Western. He had previously been a plasterer, and was currently (even as we walked in) studying to pass his exams to become a qualified embalmer. If he did pass them, he would be the only one 'in-house' at Balmer's, provided he didn't then move somewhere else where they paid better.

Balmer's used freelancers, some of whom, unsurprisingly perhaps, were pretty strange characters. None of them were medical students subsidising their studies like my mate had been. Most were already connected with the funeral trade in some way, like John, and had taken the British Institute of Embalming exams.

"I am (I'm me)", got to number 18, 1983

The creepiest were a pair of midget lesbians, like the twin girl ghosts in The Shining, inseparable, and indistinguishable in memory; but with little in common when you compared them in the flesh, apart from their doll-like proportions and a shared fashion sense apparently drawn from those minicatalogues that come with the Sunday papers – the sort that show people who aren't OAPs dressed in OAP clothes. (And they did their ordering from the men's section.)

Creepiest of all, and also like the twins from The Shining, they never spoke, to each other (at least in public anyway); and otherwise as briefly as possible, only ever one at a time, and only in response to direct questions.

I once mentioned to Dave it was a good idea not to linger in the embalming room when it was in use after we'd just left a body with them. They had already been working on another body, and the fumes from the formaldehyde were eye-watering. The room was tiny, with a low ceiling, and the only ventilation was through a minuscule extractor fan intended for a shower booth set in the skirting board in one corner.

> "You don't want to hang around in there. It's bloody bad for you. Formaldehyde's terrible stuff – it gives you cancer. God knows what it'll do to them, in there for hours at a time with their noses stuck in it."

Dave paused and raised his eyebrows:

> "Oh yeah? Health and Safety, eh? Well we'd better tell the Twisted Sisters."

We were just on our way through the front door, but Dave turned round and went straight back in. As we emerged from the corridor and reappeared in the doorway of the embalming room, they both looked up.

They were both still working on the same body, and you just knew that they'd do that until it was finished before both starting work on the other body. No division of labour there.

"Bob's got something to tell you."

Thanks very much, I thought, that makes me look like some kind of know-it-all busybody.

"Erm, yeah, it's about the fumes in here – they're really bad for your health. You can get cancer."

They both stared at me in complete silence for some seconds, then lowered their gaze and carried on where they'd left off. Dave looked at me, winked, then walked past me as he led the way out.

They weren't the only women embalmers, and you get more and more women funeral directors these days. My aunt on my dad's side used to lay people out (as an enthusiastic amateur, in a role always occupied by just such an enthusiastic amateur female in working class communities then): wash them, bung up their orifices with cotton wool, dress them, close their eyes, comb their hair. She was fascinated by death and dead bodies, in a kind of star-struck way that other women had for weddings.

She actually used to say:

"He made a lovely corpse."

She'd have loved to be an embalmer.

II

History of Embalming

Embalming is often presented as part of the funeral package, as a completely standard component like a coffin or flowers, almost as if stinting on this would somehow not be doing justice to the memory of your loved one:

> "And you will be wanting the embalming treatment." (no question mark at the end there).
>
> "Well, I don't know…"
>
> "We do recommend it – it's more hygienic." (quickly, with a similarly brief flash of a sad smile that says 'You don't want to know about what'll happen if you don't have it.')

There may also be a fuzzy impression, perhaps, that this is something like the treatment the pharaohs got, or what keeps Lenin and Ho Chi Minh looking as if they're just taking a break from affairs of state.

This taps into a surprisingly pervasive unthought-through idea at the back of people's minds that the body, or its vicinity, is still somehow passively inhabited by the personality of the deceased:

> "Ooh I couldn't have him cremated – I'd hate to think of him being burnt up like that."

Or:

"I couldn't bear to think of her buried – she hated the cold and the damp."

The idea of someone hibernating underground in their coffin like some kind of latter-day King Tut doesn't just fly in the face of everything every modern religion, not to say commonsense, tells us, it presumes that what your undertaker does will make that possible.

But there's scant similarity between what he (or she) does and what we might call ceremonial embalming.

Old Time Religion

The first Egyptian mummies probably came about by accident, from burying bodies in hot dry sand with no covering, or hunched up in a clay funerary urn – the most famous of those being *Bilanben*, from the dynasty known as the 'Flowerpot'.

Later on, it became important to the Egyptians to preserve their rulers, originally because of a belief that the body was a kind of operational base for the pharaoh's souls (five in all) to use their influence with the gods in the afterworld to keep the sun rising and the crops growing in this world. The rulers needed their attendants and servants, so they had to be preserved too, and the priests, and the civil servants.

Eventually, everyone who could afford it wanted to be preserved. Cities were built to house the dead, and the living devoted more and more time and energy to looking after the needs of the dead, building pyramids and tombs, and leaving supplies of food, drink and gifts at the tombs.

Brain Drain

To begin with, they just wrapped the body in a shroud, or bandages soaked in resin and pitch, but over time a more effective method was developed. This involved removing the internal organs (including the brain, via the nostrils or the eye sockets, with implements like long crochet needles) and then packing the body inside and out in a kind of dry marinade of mineral salts called natron, found where prehistoric lakes had dried up. This had the same effect as the original desert burials, of removing all the water from the body. Without water, the bacteria that rot the body can't survive.

The high point for Egyptian embalming was the 18th dynasty, 1555-1350BC, for the likes of Tutankhamun and Nefertiti. Mummies from this era are the best preserved, and it seems that their embalmers made some variations from the methods used either side of this period. This was only worked out very recently by a British archaeological chemist called Stephen Buckley, who got there by a combination of detective work (literally, he used gas chromatography, just like the cop shows on TV) and personal experimentation.

He was x-raying lots of mummies using new medical equipment that gave better results than anyone had seen before, and he noticed two things that were different about mummies from the 18th dynasty – two things, in fact, that shouldn't have been there. First of all, a lump rattling around in the back of the skull that looked like it might be a dried-up 3,500 year-old brain, and then there were flakes of some kind of mineral embedded throughout the flesh.

You see, according to Herodotus:

"First with a crooked iron tool they draw out the brain through the nostrils, extracting it partly thus, and partly by pouring in drugs; and after this with a sharp stone of Ethiopia they make a cut along the side and take out the whole contents of the belly, and when they have cleared out the cavity and cleansed it with palm wine they cleanse it again with spices pounded up: then they fill the belly with pure myrrh pounded up and with cassia and other spices except frankincense, and sew it together again.

Having so done they keep it for embalming covered up in natron for seventy days but for a longer time than this is not permitted to embalm it; and when the seventy days are past, they wash the corpse and roll its whole body up in fine linen cut into bands."
The History of Herodotus Book II, Macaulay translation, 1890.

Herodotus was a Greek historian, and he was writing in 450BC, but there are hieroglyphics from earlier periods showing the same sort of things he described (although sometimes the brain was removed through the eye sockets – perhaps easier because the skull is paper-thin there).

So if the lumps inside the skulls were brains, then the 18th Dynasty embalmers weren't following the usual procedure, and when Dr. Buckley analysed the strange flakes that were in the flesh, they turned out to be crystals of the mineral salts found in natron. If they were actually embedded throughout the flesh like nuts in nougat, it meant that the bodies hadn't simply been laid in a bed of dry natron, as described by Herodotus.

Long pig

Dr. Buckley favours a hands–on approach to his research, or to begin with in this case, perhaps, trotters-on – he first experimented with dead piglets to see if laying them in dry natron could get the crystals under the skin and into the flesh, and when it couldn't, he used pig's trotters in 194 separate experiments with different strengths of natron solution and different combinations of herbs and spices until he got it right. Pork is very similar, it seems, to human flesh.

He found that the concentration of natron needed to leave crystals in the flesh also tended to burn the skin off. This was where the spices that Herodotus mentioned came in – a coating of the resins and oils from the spices protected the skin and preserved the external features.

Being a man who does things properly, Dr Buckley then looked for a volunteer for the ultimate test of his theories, and found a 61 year old Torquay cabbie called Alan Billis. He was dying of lung cancer, and both he and his wife were happy with him providing posthumous input to the cause of archaeological understanding in this unique way – his wife said that she'd be the only person in the world who's got a mummy for a husband.

When he died Alan was taken to the Medico-Legal Institute in Sheffield where Dr. Buckley and an expert on ancient Egyptian funerary practice called Joann Fletcher advised the medical staff how to go about it.

The pathologist, Peter Vanezis, was surprisingly game, his first challenge being to extract Alan's internal organs through the six inch slit between the left hip and ribcage specified by his expert advisors, while yet managing to leave the heart in place – a considerable test of his dexterity, tenacity of grip, and knowledge of anatomy by touch.

I don't think it counts as cheating exactly, but they did make a few concessions to modernity – the coating of resins and oils was applied with an industrial spray gun, for instance.

High temperatures and zero humidity not cropping up too often in the weather forecast for Sheffield, they dried the body off from the natron bath in a room with the air conditioning set to replicate the Valley of the Kings. In a tribute to the irresistible power of nature, even though the body was kept behind closed doors in a windowless room in a modern climate-controlled building, they found two maggots on it at one point.

The whole experiment was completely successful – the facial features were recognisably Alan's, and the tissues retained elasticity while displaying the embedded mineral crystals seen in the 18th Dynasty mummies. When they x-rayed the head, the brain was in the same place at the back of the skull, and with the same appearance Dr Buckley had originally noticed in Egypt.

What I'd like to know is what they're going to do with Alan's mummy now – for the time being it will be stored at the Medico-Legal Institute, but it's hard to imagine that'll still be there in three and a half thousand years' time. Seems a shame to go to all that trouble, when you know the job you've done has that kind of potential, and not give it a chance stay the course.

Ship it somewhere where they have the same kind of desert conditions as Egypt? But then again, with global warming, perhaps the desert will come to Sheffield.

Alan's mummy could in theory be much more durable than some of the relative youngsters among his predecessors in Egypt. The embalming got progressively less effective from the 19th dynasty onwards, as the procedures became less and less thorough and more and more symbolic; until by the time Egypt became part of the Roman Empire in 30BC, it seems the bandaging and the decoration of the coffin were more important than how well the body inside would last.

Similar levels of care and effort to those of the 18th dynasty have been applied to other bodies than Alan's since standards declined in Egypt, but the motives have tended to be political rather than religious in those more recent times.

The method the Russians have used on Lenin, Stalin, Ho Chi Minh, and other personalities whose cult needed extending, along with the variant used for Eva Peron, is the Rolls Royce of modern embalming treatments.

Although done in the service of totalitarian political regimes, it's actually a continuation of the traditions for royal or state funerals dating from medieval times, when the body needed to lie in state for some time, and perhaps go on a farewell tour round the country.

This was originally performed by monks, the ones who normally did the butchering for the abbey. Methods varied, as did the effectiveness of the results, but best practice involved removing the soft organs (but if the brain was removed, rather than using the nose, the crown of the head would be sawn off), washing out the blood and body fluids, and using a pickling solution.

We can presume the pickling solution was made by the monks working in the kitchen (refectory?), using skills they had learnt preserving food. Typical ingredients include wine, vinegar or spirits, pickling salts and herbs and spices.

When it works, pickling can work very well indeed. A scientific study found nitrite pickling salts and alcohol were better than formaldehyde for embalming (*Nitrite pickling salt as an alternative to formaldehyde for embalming in veterinary anatomy--A study based on histo- and micro-biological analyses*, Janczyk, P et al, 2011).

The science goes like this (but because the monks didn't understand the science, their results were hit and miss, and the misses could miss by a very large margin, as we shall see):

Pickling salts in the right concentration could remove water from the body by osmosis: if the pickle is more concentrated than the solution inside the body tissues, there would be a gradient across the cell walls, and just as gravity tends to make things on gradients level off, osmosis would make water move out of the cells to dilute the stronger solution outside the body. (Osmosis means freshwater fish never stop pissing because they need to get rid of all the water that comes into their bloodstreams through their gills, blood being thicker than water.)

Dehydrating the body kills the bacteria that cause decomposition.

The pickle gets into the body by diffusion, which works in the other direction to osmosis: because the solution in the body is less concentrated, molecules of pickle move across a concentration gradient to where it's less crowded in the body tissues.

The pickle is too acid for most bacteria to live in, and ethanol (alcohol) is poisonous, as are chemicals in the herbs and spices.

The Russians get the same result by first of all removing the organs and injecting formalin, which is a solution of 40% formaldehyde normally used as an antiseptic. Formaldehyde is a caustic (too alkaline for bacteria to live in) chemical used to preserve scientific specimens. It replaces the water in the tissues. After that, they soak the body in different chemicals in a glass bath (glass, because formaldehyde reacts with metal).

Here's the recipe if you want to try it yourself: first 3% formaldehyde, then alcohol, water, glycerine, potassium acetate and quinine chloride. The Russians call what the body finishes up floating in "balsam". After that, everything except the bits that show is wrapped in rubber bandages so the stuff doesn't leak out. Twice a week they smear more balsam on the face and hands, then every 18 months it goes in the bath again (minus the bandages).

There was a bit of learning on the job with Lenin (overseen by "The Committee for Immortalisation"), but after Stalin, they had it down to a fine art, and it was rolled out anywhere there was a personality with a bereft cult: Bulgaria, Mongolia, Czechoslovakia, Angola, Guyana, Vietnam, North Korea, and more recently Hugo Chavez in Venezuela.

Suffering from hot flushes (1)

It certainly works – Lenin's been on show since 1924. There was something in the papers recently about Lenin getting mould on his face because they were strapped for cash and the procedures weren't kept up, and a junior lab tech pouring boiling water over him and "blistering" the skin. It's all rubbish. First off, his skin wouldn't blister as if he were still alive. Blistering is caused by water in the tissues heating up through contact with heat and expanding so fast it damages cell walls. There's no water in Lenin's skin. Second, there's been no cash flow problem since the collapse of Communism, because the lab was quickly sought out by a new high-spending niche market: Russian mafia. They keep another group who used to be kept busy on Lenin's behalf in business too: monumental masons.

Suffering from hot flushes (2)

By all accounts, though, the Spanish doctor who embalmed Eva Peron used a slightly different technique. Following injection of alcohol through the circulatory system (in at an artery, out from a vein), glycerine at 45°C was pumped in until it had replaced all the fluid that was originally in the tissues, which then set as it cooled down – like a South American politician-sized helping of butcher's brawn. Then, apparently over a year, Dr Ara worked on infusing paraffin wax into "certain areas of the body" and a layer of wax over the whole body.

According to a silversmith who was engaged to make a Tutankhamun-style body mould to go on top of her crystal casket, this involved suspending the corpse vertically. He doesn't specify, but we can guess this would be head-down, like a giant blonde bat.

Evita in her crystal casket was to be the centrepiece of a copy of Les Invalides, and on the anniversary of her death every year the lid would be raised and the body displayed, like that of a saint in a cathedral. I like to think they might perhaps have also installed a breathing motor under her blouse, like the Sleeping Beauties in the seaside waxworks of my childhood.

What happens at the local undertaker's is a lot less permanent and very much quicker.

Join the Jet Set

It might start with something that features in the mental image that pops into your head when North Sea oil rigs are mentioned.

Let me explain: when you die, the cells in the lining of your stomach and gut stop making the mucous that stops your stomach and gut from being digested by their own digestive juices. But the digestive juices carry on working. The sphincter valves at either end of the stomach also open, and depending on the individual anatomy and the way the body's lying, the stomach's hydrochloric acid can leak into the gut and oesophagus and damage their thin walls.

At the gut end, bacteria resident in the gut get to work on the part-digested intestines, surrounding tissue and organs, and any food that might have been in transit, which is why a greenish flush here, below the ribs, is often the first sign of decay after death; in plucked gamebirds at the butcher's just as much as bodies laid out at the undertakers. The digestive juices also attack the rest of the intestines, of course, but without the stomach acid, the walls remain intact for longer, and the bacteria are contained.

Putrefactive bacteria make gases, which then collect at the same place. This can make corpses belch or groan as a build up of gas is released through the gullet and goes past the vocal chords. This means that bodies sometimes grunt when you get hold of them to move them – definitely Uncanny Valley territory. You may have heard of bodies sitting upright, belching, and then lying down again, but I've never spoken to anyone who's seen that, in a morgue or an undertaker's. It doesn't make sense – having a belly full of gas would bend them the other way.

The main tool of the undertaker's embalmer is a long hollow needle called a trocar, which is used to suck out body fluids and pump in embalming fluid. Unlike the other methods of embalming, the soft organs are not removed. Instead, the trocar is stuck deep into the body repeatedly through the same entrance point, but each time in a different direction, to drain the gut and the contents of different parts of the body.

The point of entry is just under the sternum, at the bottom of the strip of gristle where your ribs meet, the same place that putrefactive gas builds up. Which is how, sometimes when a body's not too fresh, the connection between embalming and oil rigs comes in.

The trocar is removed from the tube connecting it to the collecting bottle and aspirating pump, and, in a bravura display similar to a chef flambéeing an entrée, jabbed vertically into the plexus, simultaneously using a cigarette lighter to ignite the escaping gas to produce a roaring blue flame sometimes several feet in height. Very impressive in a darkened room, and, as I say, curiously reminiscent of night time views of the North Sea oilfields when the rigs are flaring off their excess gas.

After any flaring off that may be necessary, and after a trocar connected to the suction pump has drained the heart, lungs, stomach, gut and bladder; 'cavity fluid' (formalin) is pumped in through the trocar using the same point of entry, followed by less concentrated embalming fluid the same way the Russians used – in through the carotid artery at the side of the neck, and out through a vein in the ankle, or through the jugular vein, which lies next to the carotid.

Like flushing a radiator.

I once saw Damien Hirst on TV, preparing one of his trademark sliced-up dead animals like some kind of Frankenstein/TV chef cross. He was standing chest-deep in a vat of formaldehyde with half a cow, wearing a big grin and a one-piece diving suit, jabbing a disposable hypodermic into the carcass, surrounded by discarded hypos floating on the surface.

If that really is how he does it, rather than a bit of typical show off pose-striking for the camera; number one, he wants to wear a gasmask, and number two, it's no wonder his pickled livestock and sharks fall to bits after a few years – he wants to use the radiator flush method and do the job properly.

Plastic Fantastic

There is a kind of ultimate, super-modern method of embalming, which, without our un-Victorian taboo on death, might have appeared in the optimistic predictions of children's comics of the last century that always began

"In the year 2000", and continued:

"we will…

…go to work in a hover car / not need to go to work because we'll all work from home using TVs that you talk to,

…eat food in tablet form that contains all the nutrition and vitamins we need / have our food cooked instantly by silver-clad mums in space-age kitchens where the furniture rises up out of the floor".

Yes, and offices will be paperless.

This sci-fi embalming technique is plastination, invented by Dr Gunter von Hagens. Dr von Hagens is a colourful character who is also famous for doing live dissections on UK national TV despite being told it's against the law (no charges brought), and for answering accusations of body snatching in various courts around the world (as director of his company, not personally, and again not guilty, I hasten to add). He also gets accused of bad taste and offences in the area of kitsch, like using dissected bodies to recreate scenes from Bond films for his '**2007**' display for 2007.

He invented plastination for medical specimens of organs and tissue used for teaching purposes, and scaled-up the technique for whole body preservation – usually human, but also horses, a gorilla, and even a giraffe. The bodies are dissected and posed to display different anatomical systems, often with the skin and muscles cantilevered out like the 3D exploded diagrams that come with manufacturer's assembly instructions.

He sometimes copies poses from historic anatomical treatises – like the flayed man holding out his skin, as if over the cloakroom counter of a very severe S&M club – and sometimes uses similar ideas of his own, like the man running so fast his skin and muscles are being peeled off by the slipstream and flapping in his wake.

As well as pinching ideas from Vesalius, he always wears a black hat in public, even when dissecting, like Rembrandt in his painting of the Syndics of Utrecht – the one with the staff of the medical school dissecting a body with the artist stage right.

Although, despite his hat, the professor doesn't claim to be any kind of artist, he is a top class anatomist, and along with the hat, he has something else in common with the great artists of history: like the renaissance master painters doing the hands and faces after their apprentices had filled in the rest of the canvas, he does the hardest bits of dissection himself.

His method of preservation is the best anyone's come up with so far, and it probably can't be bettered. All the water and fats are removed from the tissues and replaced by plastic, hard or soft, as end-product application requires. Natural colour and texture can be retained, and the weight of the specimen remains the same. Tissue or organ samples, or whole bodies, can be sliced like bacon, as thin as a sheet of paper.

First of all, the specimen or body is soaked in a bath of acetone at minus 25°C and then gradually warmed to room temperature, until first the water boils off, then the fat. Then it goes in a plastic solution (silicone, epoxy or polyester polymer), which over days or weeks is brought to the boil in a vacuum, until plastic has leached in to replace the acetone as it evaporated out. The plastic is then cured using gas, heat or UV light depending on the type used. Different plastics give different properties, in different degrees: flexibility, colour contrast or transparency.

The finished article is immune to decay, and will never fade, shrink or dry out.

Because your local embalmer's efforts are more perfunctory than the aforegoing methods, and because the typical English grave is a lot damper than the Egyptian desert, there's not much chance of there being anything for a future Howard Carter to find. In a classic case of history repeating itself; just as in the days of the pharaohs, embalming has become less thorough and more symbolic. ("What we learn from history is that we don't learn from history" – Stephen Buckley excepted of course).

One benefit that the undertaker's method has over best practice though, is the use of a pink tint in the embalming fluid, which imparts a disconcertingly healthy-looking rosy glow. You see the same thing in carbon monoxide poisoning, which is what you die of when you rig your car up as a fume trap to commit suicide. The carbon monoxide bonds better with the haemoglobin in the blood than oxygen (which is why it kills you), so it's a kind of super healthy glow, of the type produced by a brisk walk in a strong wind in nippy weather – very out of place on a corpse.

As well as improving the complexion, it also fills the tissues out, often not just getting rid of the hollow-cheeked desiccated look that corpses have, but actually making someone look better than they did before they died.

Higher pressure injecting can even get rid of wrinkles, and this – along with the make-up, wash 'n' brush up, shampoo and set (literally, since embalming fluid sets the body like rigor mortis), cotton wool inside the cheeks and eyecaps under the lids that fill the sockets out as well as keep the eyes closed – can make someone look not just better than they did before they died, but better than they had for years. The embalmer can put a smile on your face too – running a thread through the upper and lower lips to keep the mouth shut also allows him to tension it and tie it off to get any expression he likes, which the embalming fluid then helpfully freezes.

Men get a final shave of course, and here I can deal with (I was going to say 'lay to rest') another myth about dead bodies that people like to tell each other: your hair does NOT go on growing after you're dead.

It looks as if beard stubble has grown after death because the stubble that was there at death looks longer afterwards, caused by the face flesh shrinking, leaving more of the stubble exposed.

I can also state with absolute certainty, from personal observation, that the head hair does not keep growing until it fills the coffin, another one I've heard a few times.

III

Tales from the Crypt

I know this from a time when I helped move coffins in a church crypt. They had to be moved from one part of the crypt to another, stacked up, and walled in. The builders who were doing work in the crypt were too superstitious to touch them, so I, being known to be unbothered by moving bodies around because of working for Balmer's, along with a few other unsuperstitious types with strong backs that the vicar knew, spent a Saturday afternoon humping old coffins around.

Nowadays everyone would be worried about smallpox and anthrax spores, or lead poisoning from the oxides on the lead shells, but no-one bothered about that type of thing then. We wore gloves and white noddy suits like forensic technicians at a crime scene, and I taped the legs of mine to the tops of my boots, but that was it; no gasmasks or goggles or inoculations, or anything like that. As far as I know, none of us suffered any ill-effects.

You can imagine what it was like, dark, cold and clammy, even though it was a hot summer's day outside. The end of the crypt where the builders had been working had high vaulted ceilings and the walls had been whitewashed. Workbenches and parts of the walls there were illuminated by tungsten lights on stands, and the floor was covered with loops of yellow wires from the lights and black ones from the power tools; but the space we were in was dark and claustrophobic, split up into bays with low arched ceilings either side of a central passageway.

The floor was flagged, and in the confined space our boots seemed to make a lot of noise scraping on the grit and bits of rubble from the connecting wall that the builders had knocked down to discover the coffins. I can remember being conscious that our breathing seemed to make a lot of noise, too – after we got going we were breathing hard because it was hard work, mainly because of the confined spaces we were forced to work in.

Some of the coffins were really crammed in, piled on top each other anyhow, stacked right up to the ceiling, and some of them were burst or broken. It looked like the burial services were probably done in the more presentable end of the crypt where the builders were working, with the coffins then being put in place reverentially in the tidy end of the bit we were in. Then, at a later date when space was running out, the earlier arrivals were shunted away to the back so that the bays at the other end could be re-used. In any case, the oldest coffins were the ones piled up at the back. They dated from the late 18th to mid 19th centuries. We knew that because they had coffin plates with dates on, lead (or perhaps it was pewter, it was difficult to tell because they were usually badly oxidised), but some were brass, particularly on the newer ones.

The older coffins were plainer, presumably reflecting the more elegant Regency preference for uncluttered Classicism, with the newer ones showing a growing elaboration of ornament in the coffin furniture and decoration of the exterior as Victorian taste took hold. A kind of record of changing tastes as plain as that in, for instance, car design – think of the increasing use of ornament and chrome in the post-war period.

The best quality had a mummy-shaped airtight lead inner shell with soldered seams, an inner coffin of what I believe was elm, and an outer coffin of oak. Cheaper versions had only one coffin of elm. The less elaborate versions also tended to be coffin-shaped, while the others were usually (but not always) rectangular – that is to say, strictly speaking, caskets.

The exterior of the caskets, and some coffins, was covered with cloth, either something like worsted or thin felt, or what might have been velvet. Some were maroon or brown, others black or faded purple. Some looked as if they might originally have been a deep red or very dark blue, rather than maroon or purple. The cloth was held in place by rows of upholsterer's tacks, the type with the dome-shaped head; just round the edges on the older ones, but with increasingly elaborate geometric patterns as time went on, with close-set rows of three or four lines of tacks along the edges, and inbetween, single lines of window-pane check or lozenge patterns.

The older ones didn't always have handles, just rings, but the later ones usually did, and more and more floridly ornamented, as was the plate with the name and dates on it. Some had flowers on top; very sad remnants after all those years.

…'res' as in 'resting place', rather than 'residence'

As I said, some of the coffins were broken, perhaps deliberately, so that they took up less space when they were moved to a less des res, and others broke when we moved them. That's how I know there were different layers, and what the bodies looked like. The lead shell was often very brittle, and perhaps there was some kind of gas or liquid seepage from it that affected the wood of the coffin too.

The bodies were always dressed in shrouds made of thick wool that were a foot or two too long, and sometimes with a kind of snood or extravagantly long collars at the other end. I believe this custom came about originally because of a law passed by Charles II that all corpses were to be buried in a woollen shroud specifically of this generous size, a law introduced to protect the English wool trade. The priest had to mark the burial with an "A" in the parish records to Affirm that he had checked there was a woollen shroud. The only exceptions were plague victims or those buried naked because they were too poor to afford a shroud. The penalty otherwise was a fine of £5 in the local Magistrate's Court; so only the very poor, the very rich, or the very unlucky went to their grave without a shroud.

The occupants always had their hands crossed on their chest; and with the swaddling effect of the shroud, often the hands and face alone were all that was visible, with the features framed in folds of the coarse wool that filled the space between the face and the coffin edge.

Many were surprisingly well-preserved, and one or two, exposed when the lead shell collapsed as we moved them, really did look as if they had only died recently; but in those cases exposure to fresh air (comparatively speaking) and oxygen made them degrade very rapidly, in a matter of minutes. (but not 'right before your very eyes' like the kind of time-lapse photography effect that horror films use).

Others that had obviously been exposed for some time frequently retained their hair, even when there was no flesh left on the rest of the skull. This gave the appearance of a skull with a wig glued in place, and if it was a man with sideburns (although, incidentally, none had sideburns below the cheekbone), these would be curling up, as if the glue had dried up round the edges.

And I can confirm definitively, and, I hope, once and for all, that none of them had long hair filling the coffin, and the men did not all sport luxurious post-mortem beards.

The hair was often a curious orangey shade of red, like the colour that you see on Moslem men who've gone white but dye their hair and beard with henna. This was, I think, not because more people had red hair then, but some kind of post-mortem effect, perhaps something to do with chemical changes related to how the lead oxides from the shells react with body fluids.

Speaking of which, in the shells that broke open when we moved them, the bodies would usually be well-preserved, with flesh, eyebrows, and hair, and retaining some fullness in the facial features, but always with an inconvenient extra: half a pint or more of a sweet-smelling dark-coloured liquid collected in the bottom of the shell. I say inconvenient because if you happened to be lifting the coffin when it split, the liquid would spill over you. I once got some in the face when we were lifting a coffin from the top of a stack.

I can only guess it was a kind of distillate of the body fluids, the rest of them perhaps having leaked out through the soldered seams as the shell oxidised.

This substance is mentioned by John Aubrey in his *Brief Lives*. John Aubrey was a Restoration historian (although they called themselves Antiquarians then). He was generally sneered at by later historians for just being a glorified gossip who never finished anything; but he was the first person to work out that Avebury prehistoric stone circle was a prehistoric stone circle, and he was also the first person to suggest that Stonehenge was a lot older than anyone had previously suggested it was.

"John Colet (1466-1599).

John Colet, D.D., deane of St. Paula's London – vide Sir William Dugdale's Historie of Paule's church. After the conflagration his monument being broken, his coffin, which was lead, was full of a liquour which conserved the body. Mr Wyld and Ralph Greatorex tasted it and 'twas of a kind of insipid tast, something of an ironish tast. The body felt, to the probe of a stick they thrust into a chinke, like brawne. The coffin was of lead and layd in the wall about three feet above the surface of the floore."
Brief Lives ed. Rev Andrew Clark, 1898

The conflagration being the Great Fire of London in 1666, Colet had been stewing in his own juices for 67 years when Messrs Wyld and Greatorex sampled them.

What were they doing prodding poor old Colet with a stick and tasting his liquor?

Ralph Greatorex was an inventor and scientific instrument maker, and Edmund Wylde was an MP and civil servant, and the reason they were poking around St Paul's as if it was a sale of fire-damaged goods was also how John Aubrey knew them: they were all members of the Royal Society, the first professional organisation in the world for what are now called scientists (although they called themselves Natural Philosophers then.)

You might also want to know what "brawne" is, too, it seems to be an old-fashioned idea on its way to being a bygone. It's a kind of savoury jelly with the debris from cutting ham or joints or whatever embedded in it: meat leftovers in aspic.

Not *'Scotland's Other National Drink'*...

So: hair doesn't grow after death, and bodies in lead shells produce a liquor that tastes 'ironish'.

IV

British eccentricity, Yankee ingenuity

No matter how often undertakers and the British Institute of Embalmers may say so, embalming is not "a hygienic procedure", in that it makes the environment safe from what might be some kind of noxious infection associated with corpses. What it does do is make sure there won't be any smells or leakage from a body (although undertakers also line coffins with the stuff disposable nappies are made from, just in case).

As we've seen, historically it was part of the funeral process for the royal, the rich and the famous. Other attributes of upper echelon funerals would come to find their way into common funeral practice as supplied by undertakers, as I'll explain later, but for the funeral industry, embalming had an another attraction besides its preservative qualities.

The white-coated cod medical pretensions of the modern practice of embalming are central to the invention of funeral directing as a 'profession', and to the efforts of the industry to distance itself from the trade of undertaking and its embarrassing connections with jobbing joiners. That began in the United States, but it soon found its way over here.

Looking at the March 1974 issue of the *The Embalmer* - THE OFFICIAL JOURNAL OF THE BRITISH INSTITUTE OF EMBALMERS (their capitals, and in smaller letters: "A BI-MONTHLY MAGAZINE

DEVOTED TO FURTHERING THE INTERESTS OF EMBALMING THROUGHOUT THE WORLD" – and notice that's "Embalming", not "Embalmers"), and doing our best not to be distracted by the adverts…

> "REDUCE PHYSICAL LABOUR and the possibility of painful & expensive back injuries.
> Let a FERNO-WASHINGTON MORTUARY COT take the strain"

or this, for an embalming kit

> "THE 'FYFE DOUGLAS' KIT complete with fluids.
> Unsurpassed in construction, accessibility and appearance."

or, bafflingly, on several levels – tense, syntax, layout, incongruity, and use of exclamation marks (and the spacing, layout and italics are all theirs)

> *Don't let today be the tomorrow*
>
> > *you worried about yesterday!*
>
> > *Hall marked fluids, successfully applied, will take care of all your embalming problems!"*

…the title of the leading article is "Should we attempt Diagnosis?" (again, their capital on the 'diagnosis').

The answer that leaps to mind is "No, it's a bit late for that by the time someone's arrived on your slab."

I won't go into detail, and I'm paraphrasing, just in case *The Embalmer* has a team of hot copyright lawyers on tap, but the first point the author makes is that "not so long ago" surgery and its practitioners were in "much the same position" as embalmers today, and embalmers have to decide whether they take up a "respected place in society as they (surgeons) have done" or go back "to oblivion".

Interesting historical interpretation, and interesting that the author takes the long view with his "not so long ago" – it's over two hundred years since the College of Surgeons of England became the Royal College of Surgeons, and five hundred since the Royal College of Surgeons of Edinburgh was incorporated.

Anyway, what matters here, it seems, is that surgeons somehow hoisted themselves up by their own bootstraps to be on the same social level as physicians, and it's time the people who squirt preservatives into dead bodies did the same. And walked the wards of hospitals, and started calling themselves doctors?

Again, I won't go into the details, but the article is full of pompous theorising and medical terminology. It consists of a list of medical conditions and their effects in gross anatomical terms.

About the only example that means an embalmer would have to do more than they normally would, except a bit more thoroughly, is uraemia (which the author spells wrong, and no, I don't mean he used the American spelling), where we're told that cerebral oedema (fluid on the brain) is so common that the brainpan should be drained using the trocar as a matter of course.

Most cases of death from uraemia would have been post mortemed, which would mean that their brain pans would have been well and truly drained when the brain was removed as part of the standard procedure, which would make this example of "diagnosis" for embalmers redundant too.

I think you get the picture: because they wear white coats and use surgical-type instruments, embalmers/funeral directors should be treated as professionals, and charge professional-type fees like white-coated surgeons do.

This theory breaks down a bit in the UK, because the embalmer is usually a badly-paid minion rather than the funeral director himself, as in the US.

How embalming for funerals got to this point is another story full of the kind of eccentric characters the history of the funeral business is full of.

Wives and Sweethearts

Arterial embalming was the invention of William Hunter, an 18th century Scottish anatomist, but the idea of using it to preserve a human body for something other than medical instruction was Martin van Butchell's, a dentist who had been one of Hunter's students.

When van Butchell's wife Maria was dying in 1775, he asked Dr Hunter to embalm her. The intention was to prepare her for display, like a medical specimen, but not to instruct medical students: to put in van Butchell's shop as a kind of conversation piece and visitor attraction. He also apparently put it about that under a clause in their wedding contract, he continued to receive payments from her parents until his wife was dead and buried.

This sounds bizarre, but it was more or less in character for van Butchell.

He was famous for, in approximate ascending order of eccentricity:

The length of his beard. He never shaved, and published pamphlets warning of the dangers to health from shaving.

Always wearing the same hat, which eventually faded from black to white, and was more holes and cracks than hat.

Including another clause in the famous wedding contract that obliged his wife to wear only black or white (including undergarments and nightgowns), and having chosen, never to wear any other colour. His first wife wore black, his second, white.

Never referring to or addressing his children by name, training them instead to respond to a series of whistles, as if they were dogs.

Carrying a large bone club on a loop attached to his wrist whenever he went out, reputedly from the island of Otaheite (the contemporary name for Tahiti), "for protection".

Going everywhere on a small white pony which he painted, sometimes with purple spots or swirls, sometimes purple with black or white spots, and sometimes just purple.

We know exactly how Maria van Butchell was embalmed, because her husband was good enough to take notes, as was Dr Hunter, and these still exist, in the archives of the Royal College of Surgeons in London.

She died at three in the morning, a sculptor came to make a death mask at eight, and at two in the afternoon Dr Hunter's assistant Dr Cruikshank turned up to inject five pints of turpentine mixed with vermillion into the crural arteries, at the top of the legs by the groin. Turpentine is distilled from pine resin, and vermillion is a red pigment made by heating mercury and sulphur together.

The next morning, Drs Hunter and Cruickshank cut open the torso and dissected the lungs and abdominal organs, assisted by van Butchell, who was able to ascertain that his wife had died of emphysema, pneumonia, and cirrhosis of the spleen and liver.

They then injected oil of turpentine mixed with camphorated spirits of wine into the major arteries.

Camphor is what eco-friendly moth balls are made of, and spirits of wine is ethyl alcohol, or ethanol, distilled from wine.

Dr Hunter's anatomy course ended with a lecture on the preparation of medical specimens, and from his own notes, also in the Royal College of Surgeons, these injections were to be made "under such pressure that the flesh became turgid", and the areas affected massaged until the pink tinge from the vermillion was spread throughout.

Powdered rosin (solidified pine resin), camphor and nitre (saltpetre or potassium nitrate) mixed with spirits of wine were then injected into the organs. The notes Dr Hunter made at the time agree with his lecture notes on technique here: the flesh and organs were first squeezed to remove every trace of fluid, and the preservative solution massaged in. The powder was also dusted over the cavity and over the organs before and after they were replaced.

The next day, van Butchell opened the abdomen again and added more rosin and camphor solution.

On the fourth day, Drs Hunter and Cruikshank returned to place the body in its display case, a box with glazed panels in the lid. After they'd put glass eyes in, and Mrs van Butchell into her wedding dress, she was laid on and in a bed of 130 lbs of dry Plaster of Paris powder, the idea of which was to absorb moisture, and was to be periodically replaced.

Before closing the case van Butchell placed three "arquebusade bottles" between his wife's thighs. An arquebus was a kind of medieval musket, and arquebusade was (and still is) a salve for cuts and bruises made from Swiss herbal essences and brandy. The arquebus was associated with Switzerland because Swiss mercenaries were early adopters of this warfare-altering technology, and presumably also spread the fame of this early antiseptic in the wars they fought in.

Arquebusade bottles had a top with a small opening like a cologne bottle that would allow the gradual release of vapour from the contents. The three bottles were filled respectively with camphorated spirits "very rich of the gum" (strong solution of rosin), oil of lavender and oil of rosemary.

Van Butchell then cemented the joints of the lid and the panes of glass in place, using a mixture of rosin glue and spirits of wine.

Van Butchell paid William Hunter 100 guineas for his services, but perhaps got this back before long from the fees he charged for viewing his wife after she was placed in his parlour. Not that he needed to – he was the most fashionable and best-paid dentist in London, despite being self-taught. That wouldn't exactly qualify as a selling point in the world of dentistry today, but apparently he had problems with his own teeth, and being the kind of man he was, went for the DIY approach.

In a world where the effectiveness of anaesthetic was indicated by its percentage over proof, having a dentist with personal appreciation of the consequences of his technique was surely an advantage.

It wasn't just about pain avoidance either – one of his tooth transplants lasted six years, a record at the time (people would pay to have someone else's teeth removed and inserted when their own were extracted, usually one of their servants).

He also sold individually-tailored hernia trusses of his own invention, and treated anal fistulas "without confinement, burning or cutting". That would definitely be the way you would want them treated, I should think.

Dr Hunter's efforts impressed John Sheldon, his assistant lecturer, enough for Sheldon to request more of the same for his mistress when she died a few months later. (Sheldon is known today as the first Englishman to fly – as a passenger in a balloon, 1784.)

While Mrs van Butchell was kept in the parlour, Sheldon kept Miss Johnson's remains in his bedroom, but she was evicted at the request of his wife when he subsequently married. Curiously enough, she eventually ended up sharing a home with Mrs van Butchell (Miss Johnson that is, not Mrs Sheldon).

After Dr van Butchell's death, their son donated his mother's remains (and her green parrot, who at some point had joined his former mistress in her display cabinet, placed between her feet) to the Royal College of Surgeons, where they became part of the collection originally started by William Hunter's younger brother John, and where the remains of Miss Johnson had already ended up.

Like William, John Hunter was a surgeon and lecturer, but at the time was best known for this collection; which aside from meticulously dissected examples of disease and anatomy, also included freaks, sports of nature, monsters and most famously "The Irish Giant", supposedly the tallest man in the world at the time.

After drinking himself to death after a career as an exhibit in a freak show, Charles Byrne wanted to be buried at sea in a (very large) lead coffin, but John Hunter's plans for his eventual fate were presumably better supported financially, and Byrne carried on his career beyond an unwatery grave in 1783 to become the hardest-working exhibit of the lot.
He even survived the German bomb that hit the Royal College of Surgeons in 1941. You can still go and see him there today (unlike Maria van Butchell, her parrot, or Miss Johnson, who all unfortunately failed to escape immolation by Göring's incendiary).

John Brown's Body

The use of arterial embalming by undertakers is today just about universal in America, and that's where to all intents and purposes it began. Like so many harbingers of modernity that are more often associated with the First World War – mass production and interchangeability of parts, machine guns, barbed wire, submarines, aerial reconnaissance, dog tags – embalming by undertakers is actually a by-product of the American Civil War. In fact, modern embalming started because of the American Civil War.

Americans weren't used to war, having been fortunate enough to more or less miss out on it since 1776, and the idea that soldiers get buried where they fall, the most practical way of doing things, and what everyone else had been doing since people started killing each other in any sort of numbers, wasn't at all popular.

They wanted their sons' and brothers' and fathers' bodies brought home and buried in the family grave after a proper funeral. Different surgeons on both sides used arterial embalming to preserve the remains to make that possible (though mainly for officers, because it was expensive), but the best at publicity was Dr Thomas Holmes, so he's the one that gets called "The Father of Modern Embalming".

By who? – lots and lots of undertakers who write histories of embalming to get letters after their names from cod academic institutions. Have a look on the internet.

Another contender

Thanks to William Hunter, the idea of arterial embalming had been around for a long time when the Civil War started, and it would have been familiar to Dr Holmes, and anyone else who'd been a medical student or worked in a hospital, because it was the standard method for preparing medical specimens. The preservatives Holmes used weren't based on William Hunter's formula, though, but those of a French chemist called Souquet, who used zinc chloride.

Souquet himself built on the work of another French chemist called Jean-Nicholas Gannal, who was the first person to suggest undertakers should embalm everyone as a matter of course on public health grounds.

M. Gannal also survived Napoleon's retreat from Moscow (escaping after being taken prisoner seven times), invented new processes for printing, refining borax and making white lead and lint, and wrote a history of embalming.

He patented embalming using aluminium salts in 1837, and his book on embalming was published in translation in the US in 1840, and he sold his patent rights to US undertakers in 1845.

Who's the Daddy?

Interestingly, French wikipedia awards him the title of "founding father of modern embalming" (le père fondateur de l'embaumement moderne), rather than Dr Holmes, with, considering the foregoing, some justification.

Unfortunately, Père Gannal's method didn't work so well, because there was no attempt to take out the body fluids as the embalming fluid went in, and aluminium salts turned out to be unreliable preservative agents.

The other reasons embalming didn't catch on with the French undertaking profession were the arsenic that he and Souquet also specified, and the fact that the treatment was expensive.

Dr Holmes in America wasn't so finicky about using arsenic, though, and removing body fluids was less of a problem because most of his subjects came handily pre-drained by the effects of modern warfare and/or battlefield surgery.

Another advantage the trade in America enjoyed was a well-developed railway system that cut down travelling time and could cope with large numbers of bodies all needing to be moved at once – Holmes alone claimed to have personally embalmed 4,028 soldiers.

Holmes made his name by embalming the first hero of the Civil War, a Colonel Ellsworth, who died in the act of removing a Confederate flag from the top of a building. It hardly counted as an act of heroism carried out under fire, because the building was in a town that was taken without opposition (until Ellsworth removed the flag).

The thing about this flag was that it was very big, and President Lincoln could see it across the river from the White House after the town it was in joined the Confederacy. Ellsworth offered to go and take it down.

It wasn't expected that Alexandria, VA would offer any resistance, and so it proved. Ellsworth only took four men with him when he went to the building with the flag, which was a hotel.

There were no problems until after Ellsworth had taken down the flag and gone downstairs with it, when the hotel owner appeared and gave Ellsworth both barrels from a double-barrelled shotgun, killing him instantly. He was then in his turn shot by one of Ellsworth's men. (And was subsequently celebrated in the South as the war's first hero in the same way that Ellsworth was by the Union.)

The whole thing was a Perfect Storm of PR: Ellsworth was a handsome young volunteer soldier already famous for two things: being such a good mate of President Lincoln's that Lincoln said he thought of him as his younger brother, and raising an American Zouave regiment inspired by the French north African troops famous for their massively baggy trousers.

Now he was the first casualty of the war, wearing an exotic uniform and carrying an 8x14 ft enemy flag he'd just cut down for the President; the man who shot him was a notorious violent slaveowner and champion of slavery; a reporter from New York happened to be on the spot; and Lincoln had the body brought to the White House to lie in state.

Ellsworth was the first casualty of the war despite the fact the war was six weeks old, and had kicked off with a full-on military engagement – 3,000 Confederate shells had been fired at Fort Sumter, all apparently without hitting anyone.

In fact, four Union soldiers had fallen before Ellsworth, but none of them in action.

Technically, of course, Ellsworth hadn't died in action either – he'd been shot by an enraged civilian rather than a member of the Confederate armed forces on the field of battle – but then neither had any of his predecessors, and none of them died in any kind of heroic or glamorous way, and none of them were officers.

The first was a gunner who was blown up by his own gun when it misfired during a hundred gun salute that the garrison at Fort Sumter fired in tribute to themselves for their "honorable surrender", and the others were Federal reservists killed in brawls with pro-Confederate mobs that attacked them when they got off a train in Baltimore on their way to Washington.

Along with everything else that it beat the First World War to, the American Civil War was also the first war that was reported as it happened, thanks to the telegraph and the introduction of the steam roller printing press (despite the immediate mental image this conjures up, it means using papier maché moulds to make metal plaques for newsprint, rather than shoving paper under the rollers of one while it goes trundling along the road).

Colonel Ellsworth and his flag must have been a godsend to newspaper editors, and Dr Holmes made sure it was a godsend to him too. He want straight to the White House and offered Lincoln to embalm his friend's body so it could lie in state in an open casket for as long as he liked, and then do the same in New York on its way home to be buried, all for free.

The fact that there was a public viewing of the colonel's body in an open casket was much commented on in the press, along with Dr Holmes's name as the genius who made it possible.

After that he never looked back. When Lincoln's twelve year old son died the next year, Holmes embalmed him, then when Lincoln himself died three years after that, Holmes got the dream embalming gig of all time.

His name also lives on because the soldiers he embalmed wore the uniform of the winning side, of course.

Post Combat Stress (and) Disorder

Hundreds of protégé embalmers paid to learn his methods and bought his portable kits and embalming fluids, and then travelled with the armies, setting up shop in their camps. Fights regularly broke out between these camp follower vultures as they squabbled over the corpses of wealthy or famous casualties – embalming for officers started at $50, and men $25, and prices increased as the war went on.

Pessimistically-minded soldiers started wearing home-made metal dog tags to make it easier for embalmers to identify their bodies in the piles of dead in the field hospitals and makeshift morgues, and the practice continued after the war.

Holmes didn't rest on his laurels. After the war he made up for the slackening off in trade by selling his patented embalming fluid to everyone else in the business (his mixture contained less arsenic than his competitors', a definite selling point from the point of view of its purveyors, even if irrelevant to the recipients).

He also became something of a recluse, preferring to spend more and more of his time in his home in the company of the embalmed bodies and body parts he gradually filled it with. His final gift to humanity was a leak-proof dual-purpose sleeping and body bag, which he advertised vigorously in his declining years, despite, to his disappointment and surprise, the public showing very little interest or appreciation.

V

Down to Earth

If you're not intending a body to lie in state for weeks or years at a time, or shipping it home from a war, embalming as a concept is fundamentally illogical – the idea of burying a body is for it to decompose; and anything that interferes with that process is counterproductive. Embalming is also bad because the formaldehyde leaches out from buried bodies into the water table, which is why in Canada and the US graves are lined with concrete or brick. It's equally pointless if you're going to cremate the body.

Embalming is in one way a hangover from a time when proper refrigeration only existed in cargo boats or warehouse cold stores, and undertakers used blocks of ice delivered by the iceman. The fact that it's difficult to chill a body quickly that way, combined with the widespread custom of laying out the body at home, meant that embalming actually was something of a hygienic necessity in those days.

It was introduced in Britain in the 1880s, but it wasn't common, perhaps because it was so expensive (costing as much as a basic funeral on its own), and it didn't really start to catch on until the 1920s. Dottridge Bros, suppliers of hearses and other undertaking kit to other undertakers, were still marketing their patented *Drikold* preservative system in the 1930s. It consisted of blocks of carbon dioxide 'dry ice' to be placed on the corpse's solar plexus.

Surprisingly, there may be one situation where embalming could still be a good idea in Britain today.

In theory, if the funeral's within 8 to 10 days, and there's to be no viewing of the body, there should be no need for embalming – hospitals and undertakers both have proper refrigeration these days.

But because of global trends in the world of big business and their effects on the funeral trade, that assumption can, in one particular combination of circumstances, be put in doubt, as I'll explain later.

Funeral directing here has always seemed to model itself on the American trade in modern times, and embalming is almost universal there, partly for historical reasons, but perhaps mainly because of their tradition of favouring burial over cremation, and their liking for open casket funerals. Embalming makes for a better-looking corpse.

They think it's something we don't do, though, strangely enough:

> "Embalming is mostly a North American practice in modern times. European corpses have the trendy 'au naturel' look."
> *A Brief History of Modern Embalming* (unattributed), National Museum of Funeral History exhibit, Houston, Tx.

But we do – and it's not just us, it's the same in France, Germany, Scandinavia, Italy, Spain and Eastern Europe.

Belief in embalming as an article of faith is necessary for members of the British Institute of Embalmers. It's number one of the five points of the "Member's Code of Ethics" which all members of the institute must be able to recite from memory, and do, whenever a new member is awarded their certificate of membership at a divisional meeting.

Altogether now...

> "I believe that the practice of Embalming is in the interest of Public Health (their capitals) and promise to promote embalming to the best of my ability".

It's also worth remembering that another traditional selling point played on the lingering persistence of a surprisingly popular (or perhaps popular isn't really the right word) Victorian obsession; the fear of premature burial. No chance of that after you've been embalmed.

In a world where medical science's understanding of coma and narcolepsy was rudimentary to nonexistent, and clinical practice was a lot more haphazard, the Victorians were perhaps right to worry about being buried alive.

'Laying out' the body at home or in the church, wakes, and vigils by the body were all just as much practical measures against this historical fear as they are part of grieving ritual.

With bells on...

The Victorians, with their can-do approach and genius for invention and gadgetry, added patented fixes from the worlds of engineering and science, based on naval technology borrowed from the ship's bridge and anticipating that of the submarine control room: the speaking tube and the periscope. A metal tube over the occupant's face communicated between the coffin and the gravesite.

In the basic model it only worked as a speaking tube (and as an outlet for the gases of putrefaction to announce when it was definitely time to remove the tube), but it was also available with the addition of a periscope at eye level up top to study the deceased's features in case of their being alive but unable to speak. A further refinement was the addition of a cord connecting one of the deceased's fingers to a bell above ground.

These devices required the services of fulltime graveyard attendants (the 'graveyard shift'), with the bell option proving problematic for those on watch because of false alarms - trapped gases could expand the abdomen of the body underground and move the finger resting on it.

Another, more popular means of addressing the possibility of premature burial, which dealt with the problem at source, was to place a knife or revolver in the corpse's hand before closing the coffin prior to burial. An idea that still has resonance in the proclamations of Charlton Heston and NRA bumper stickers...

...and ringtones

Recent times have seen a more ad hoc application of the technology of its time to the same end, and originally for the same reason. South Africans apparently share the Victorians' dread of premature burial, and started burying people's mobile phones with them. From there, the practice has spread across continents and social classes, and is now popular in the US, particularly with young people. There, the deceased's account is kept going so that friends and family can leave messages; in an updated version of the graveside soliloquy for the time-poor cash-rich.

Other Baggage on the Last Journey

Surprising quantities and varieties of accoutrements end up as landfill after being included in the coffin as modern day grave goods by grieving relatives, intended for recycling on the other side.

The common link is a closeness to the deceased's heart (or liver/addiction centre in the brain) in life: toys (the stuffed type almost as often for adults as children), booze, cigs, photos, partner's keepsakes, china mugs (the sort with "The World's Best Dad/Grandad" etc).

You see the same type of thing in the street now where someone's been hit by a car or murdered, along with condolence cards or poems and flowers (all wrapped in cellophane or laminated, in a kind of echo of the Victorian fashion for decorating graves with wax or pottery floral displays and wreaths under glass domes).

It started happening at some point in the last 15 years or so, and it's probably part of a kind of globalisation of habits and behaviour that has affected Britain; like people hugging each other more in public, punching the air to show they're happy, and being less inhibited in public generally.

It's interesting that the traffic seems to be all one way. We get less inhibited here, but there's no cooling down where emotions traditionally run higher. We get the Notting Hill Carnival, fun runs in fancy dress and St Patrick's Day parades, but I don't see train spotting or Morris Dancing taking the world by storm, and there's no sign of the curt nod of the head and muttered "Howdyerdo" replacing group hugs or air kissing in less reserved parts of the world.

Burying things with bodies doesn't make any sense at all if you're a Christian, or a Muslim, or a Jew (or if you're atheist). Is it popular because people have always done it, or because of a love of romantic gestures? Or is it because people believe more in ghosts than religions?

Either way, we can only suppose that future archaeologists will make of us just exactly what we make of the people whose graves our archaeologists dig up.

The (Red) Devils' Music

The weirdest collision of areas of faith in one funeral that I came across was that of a man in his late fifties who left very exact instructions on dress code for his last journey.

It was, unusually at that time, an open coffin job, and it had to be. One of his ruling passions was rock and roll, and he had such a fine upstanding quiff, (vertically) in death just as much as (horizontally) in life, that it projected some inches above the sides of the coffin.

Draped round the back of his neck, and laid either side of his chest in the manner of a priest's stole (or indeed in the manner that The King himself wore such scarves at his concerts in later career, before touching them to the sweat of his brow like sudaria before bestowing them on members of his audience), was a white nylon scarf with "ELVIS" printed on it.

He was also wearing a Manchester United shirt, with his hands clasped on his chest in prayer, grasping a rosary and a keyfob with a picture of Elvis on it. Tied on one wrist, a Man United scarf, the seventies incarnation, narrow, with red & white stripes lengthways, with MAN UNITED in white, no crest, no yellow detailing, worn in the way football fans did then, so that it was visible when the arm was raised; leaving the hands free for salutes or the elevated hand-clapping used to punctuate chants.

The floral decorations on the hearse roof spelled out ELVIS on one side and MAN U on the other, with a giant guitar on top, all in red and white carnations.

Speaking of sculptural floral decorations, (as I will again later) the one that's always puzzled me is the chair.
I understand the symbolism: the place at table or in front of the hearth/TV vacated; but who first thought of it, and managed to sell the idea to someone for the first time? Because it appeared in the canon of floral funeral tributes in Britain during my time. I wouldn't like to say exactly when, but it must have been sometime around the mid-eighties.

What you would *be seen dead in*

Your undertaker will provide a shroud (nylon, not wool) for burial, but they don't usually do suits or formal wear for the last formal event you'll attend (and the one you're guaranteed to be late at).

They have plenty of choice in America, though, with whole catalogues of burial wear for you to flick through. It all looks a bit flashy to British eyes, often quite literally so, because they seem to have a penchant for shiny materials in often surprisingly bright colours (look online for 'burial clothing').

...or not

Then there was the family who wanted an open coffin funeral for their grandad, but thought the price of a shroud was a bit steep.

They asked if they could hire a suit, and when the shop manager said that wasn't possible, the grandson said he had a suit that was a bit tight on him that his grandad could be buried in. Shortly afterwards he brought it in, and his grandad was dressed in it and put on view in the shop's chapel of rest.

Two days later, the grandson came back, and said he needed the suit for a job interview, so off it came, and grandad had a closed coffin funeral after all.

VI

Secrets of embalming

My personal introduction to embalming was courtesy of Maurice, boss of Balmer's, in the same spirit, I now suspect, as the little test he set me at the start of our acquaintance, which had involved me stuffing someone's grandad into his funeral outfit.

It was during my first week in the job, and I'd been sent round to Thrale's in the van with my oppo Dave for our first job of the day, but when we got there, there didn't seem to be a great deal happening. Normally, the manager would tell you where the body was and you'd get the trolley out and get on with the job straight away. He might offer you a cup of tea before you put the body on the van, if there was no hurry, but standing around doing nothing like this was normally reserved for visits that overlapped the mid-morning tea break or lunch.

Also unusually, although I didn't know that at the time, Maurice, the boss of the firm, was there, and he didn't seem to have anything particular to do or anywhere to go, either. After a while, rather than the shop manager, John, telling us what we were supposed to do, Maurice said:

> "Could you go into the back, Bob, Geoff wants to have a word with you?"

> "What about?" (and who's Geoff, I thought.)

"It's alright, he'll tell you, just go through."

The back room was, I knew, where the embalming was done, having previously collected bodies from there for delivery back to the shops where the funerals had been arranged. Just down a narrow passage from the front of the shop, it was a low-ceilinged cramped room, windowless, and with just room for two postmortem tables, with stainless steel top surfaces with runnels converging on a drainhole. The resemblance of these to a giant kitchen sink drainer of the type you stack washing up on was underlined by the fact that a black rubber tube from the drainhole discharged into a plastic washing-up bowl on a shelf underneath.

Geoff was a large Northerner in his early twenties with large but not unhandsome features and light brown curly hair that half covered his ears like a Kevin Keegan perm. He was wearing a cheesecloth shirt with the sleeves rolled up. I guessed he was from Middlesborough from his accent; north-east, but not Geordie or Wearside, and his anachronistic appearance – I knew Middlesborough football fans were famous for long hair with sidies and flares for years after they'd disappeared from the rest of the country.

He was sitting at the side of one of the tables as I came in, and he had another plastic washing-up bowl in his hands, which he put down to rub his hands together and pat his stomach appreciatively as he said:

> "Mmm, lovely! I could just do with takin' some of this home for me tea."

The washing-up bowl contained the contents of the body cavity of a grannie lying on the table, as well as, I would discover later, her brain.

Her face and hair, propped up on a black rubber neckrest above what is usually described in true crime pulp fiction as an eviscerated hulk, were incongruously unaffected and jaunty-looking, wearing, respectively, a surprised expression with garish and inappropriately youthful make-up and a cauliflower perm that looked recently applied.

I didn't faint or throw up. In fact, I wasn't bothered at all. I can remember making a mental note of the fact that, while I knew very well what I saw was real, it nonetheless seemed too much like a special effects creation from a slasher movie for me to take it seriously. In looking back, I have a curious and extraordinarily vivid recollection in which, at the same time as standing there making small talk with Geoff, I watch myself doing so from a vantage point up by the ceiling in the corner of the room, like simultaneously watching and acting in a scene from, say, The Texas Chainsaw Massacre.

After a short while, during which Geoff asked me where I was from, I discovered he was in fact from Middlesborough, and he attempted to discuss football with me, Maurice appeared in the doorway with a perky smile on his face and a manner I can only describe as 'jovial'.

"Everything alright, Bob?"

"Yes thanks, Maurice. But what was it you wanted me to see Geoff about?"

"Oh, I just thought you ought to meet him."

I'll bet you did, I thought.

"Er, ok, I see, but, was there anything else?"

"No, that was all, you can get on with it now."

After Maurice had left, and while Dave was on some self-imposed errand (more of that later) John the shop manager did some bonding.

"So you were alright were you, Bob?"

"Yes, I've never been squeamish."

"But you never really know until you've seen something like that. I remember my first time; I went as white as a sheet and I had to go and sit down. Nothing bothers me now though – road accidents, the lot. You see it all. What did you do before this?"

"Painting and decorating."

"Yeah? I used to be a plasterer. You reckon you'd be alright with a road accident?"

"No, I don't think anything like that'd bother me. The only thing I don't like the idea of is children."

At that, John's eyes lit up, and his face shone with enthusiasm.

"Right, I'll let you know next time we get a bad one in, you can come and have a look."

I found his relish for the situation off-putting and rather creepy. It was almost like a 'man of the world' looking forward to introducing an ingénue to his first taste of hard porn.

I thanked him for the offer, but said that I didn't think it would be necessary.

After I'd had time to think about this event, a disturbing thought occurred to me. While there may or may not be a necessity for embalming a particular body in the first place, selling it to someone for a body that had been post-mortemed might seem suspiciously like sharp practice – there would be no 'trunk' on the arterial tree (as it's called) that's used to distribute the embalming fluid, so it would just piss straight into the cavity where the organs used to be, and stay there.

But then again, you (or rather, Geoff) could make it work through the veins and arteries to the head, to make someone look better for an open coffin funeral, and to the individual limbs. It would take longer, of course, and embalmers don't get paid that much (maybe £20,000 a year at the most).

In all this, I must stress that this was over twenty years ago, and Balmer's were cowboys, even for those days. You don't need to worry about the body of anyone you know being kept in such squalid circumstances or treated like they were at Balmer's.

Everything is much more operating theatre-like and properly done now, for two reasons: the appearance of AIDS, and the effects of the takeover mania that's changed the face of undertaking everywhere since I worked at Balmer's.

It's still not regulated in the way that for instance food preparation or farming is – if you want to make cheese to sell, the place you make it has to be covered in stainless steel and tiles, and health inspectors come round to check it is before they'll give you a licence.

Despite the public hygiene implications and the fact that chemicals hazardous to employee health are used, there isn't even any licence for embalming suites to be inspected for compliance with.

All part of the general what-goes-on-behind-the-scenes-stays-behind-the scenes nature of undertaking, maybe; but if you work in a plywood factory where formaldehyde is used, your employers have to store it according to strict regulations and make sure you're protected when you use it, and the place would be visited by environmental health inspectors to make sure your bosses stick to the rules.

And it's not just that embalming is off the radar for environmental health inspectors; it is in fact completely unregulated.

And I've had that confirmed in black and white by the British Institute of Embalmers:

From: BIE <info@bioe.co.uk>
      Subject: **RE: Govt regulation**
Date: 6 February 2012 10:38:43 GMT
To: Robert Connolly

No embalming is not governed at all. The there are no inspections.

Ian Grainger
Administration Secretary
The British Institute of Embalmers

-----Original Message-----
From: Robert Connolly
Sent: 06 February 2012 09:50
To: enquiry@bioe.co.uk
Subject: Govt regulation

I sent an enquiry via your website last week. If a reply was sent, it didn't arrive.

Is embalming regulated by government or local government in any way? Do Environmental Health or Trading Standards Officers make visits of inspection to check standards of hygiene or storage/disposal of hazardous chemicals?

Bob Connolly

That's despite the World Health Organisation International Agency for Research on Cancer at the UN declaring formaldehyde a Class 1 carcinogen in 2009.

It's also despite the fact that a perfectly good substitute for formaldehyde as an embalming agent exists. In fact, glutaraldehyde isn't just a substitute, it's superior, both as a preservative, and for health & safety considerations.

As a preservative it's better because it doesn't cause dehydration of the tissues like formaldehyde, and it works at a lower pH. That's good because one of the factors in speeding decay is acidity (high pH) caused by the breakdown of blood products in the tissue as part of the process of rigor mortis. It also penetrates quicker, and the chemical bonding with body proteins is more stable than with formaldehyde.

That means the flesh retains its elasticity and the dyes that stop the flesh going grey circulate better.

In health & safety terms, although glutaraldehyde is a severe eye and skin irritant,

> "there is no firm evidence to indicate that long-term exposure to glutaraldehyde causes can cause harmful effects."
> Professor H. T. McKone, *Today's Chemist at Work*, December 2002, p.34, published by the American Chemical Society.

To cap it all, glutaraldehyde is a better disinfectant than formaldehyde; the very thing embalmers make the most of in making their case for embalming.

It's been around for a while, too: it was first used as a substitute for formaldehyde in 1955.

So why haven't undertakers switched to it in all those years, for their employees' health and for the sake of the environment, if not because it works better?

Because, litre for litre, it costs five times more than formaldehyde (but on the other hand, because it's more effective, they'd use less of it).

And if all the weight of evidence against using formaldehyde wasn't enough, in 2007 the EU banned its use as a biocide, specifically including embalming.

An Englishman's Embalming Suite is His Castle

How can this be? How can the funeral business buck all that scientific evidence and health and environment legislation and continue using formaldehyde when it's illegal?

Because the British Institute of Embalming has successfully lobbied the EU for the undertaking trade to be exempted on "cultural grounds".

And what part of the proud heritage of our scepter'd isle is it, specifically, that dictates bodies must be embalmed with formaldehyde, as part of the time-honoured customs and usage of the roast beef-eating, sound of leather on willow-loving Brit?

The Irish Wake of course! The whole of Britain must be exempted because of the tradition of the Irish wake, which has the body in an open coffin at the centre of it.

In Ireland. Which isn't part of the UK.

Yes, I know Ulster is, and I know that migration and intermarriage means there is a large Irish element in the British cultural mix, but I think we can be pretty sure that open coffin wakes held in the living room of the deceased don't really figure too much in the manifestation of that rich cultural heritage in the UK today.

And how come you've not read or heard anything about all this?

Once again, it's because we as a society are whatever the equivalent of prudish is in this context, in the way the Victorians were prudish about sex. Squeamish isn't the right word, it's more a conspiracy to separate death as far as possible completely from life and keep it well out of sight.

People used to grow up experiencing friends and relatives dying at home, in the same way that births took place at home, so that death used to be a part of life.

People don't die at home now (or if they do, they usually die on their own, and there's no wake): they die *in* a home, or at a hospital, and no-one sees the body, just a box going through curtains or into a grave at some later point.

And the cremation is censored and the grave is bowdlerised, with the earth being hidden from sight by the kind of artificial grass you see in greengrocers' displays – the same way that the Victorians (apparently) used to thwart a bawdy glimpse of a piano leg's ankle with a macramée fetlock.

So it's not surprising that goings on in the funeral business don't often appear in the pages of your daily paper (except, I've noticed, for "and finally" type stories in The Daily Mail about people, usually in America, being buried on their motorbike or having Doritos mixed with their ashes – which, by the way, was the inventor of Doritos, Arch West, under the headline "Goodbye Mr Chips").

Anyway, to return to my point about embalming being different now: precisely which corporate developments allow me to say so confidently that the totally unregulated funeral business of today doesn't have any squalid Dickensian-style embalming suites (or practices) like Balmer's did?

The answer is that the same takeover mania that affected the rest of the business world in the 80s happened in the funeral business too.

First it was the French PFG (Pompes Funèbres Générales) snapping up sleepy olde worlde British undertaker's shops, then it was an American company, one of the biggest in the world that you've never heard of, called SCI (Service Corporation International) of Houston, Tx. (That's pronounced 'Hewston' in Texas, but 'Hooston' everywhere else in America. So now you know. And Las Vegas is 'Loss' Vegas, perhaps quite appropriately for most visitors.)

Funnily enough, PFG had previously 'Americanized' the French funeral trade in the 1950s, introducing embalming and Funeral Parlors for the display of the body, commercialising something previously managed by the family and a female 'layer out' (ensevelisseuse); and although that had all happened much earlier in Britain, there was one aspect of the American business model that didn't make it across the Atlantic to here.

Undertakers in France were originally joiners who went on from just making the coffin to providing the 'pompe' for the 'funèbre' ('pompe funèbre' = French for 'undertaker') by selling black crape drapery and decoration for the home and providing hearses and professional mourners, in Imperial France much as they did in Victorian Britain.

For some reason though, while British undertakers Americanized their services to the public 30 years earlier than the French, they continued to display less appetite for New World get-up-and-go within the trade itself.

So, while the French trade was slower in being Americanized, when it was, PFG went the whole hog and applied the same brisk, hard-nosed business mentality across the board, treating other undertakers as competitors rather than mates, undercutting prices, making offers and buying them up until they had a virtual monopoly.

However, after the British stock market was deregulated in the 80s and PFG did the same thing here, PFG didn't have it their own way for very long. They turned out to be just the warm-up act for SCI of America, because when PFG's publicly-traded share of the British funeral market became big enough to be interesting to SCI, it was duly swallowed up by SCI, and more besides.

The SCI empire in Britain is now British owned, and has no connection with the parent company, although, confusingly, it's still called Dignity, just like SCI's funeral brand in America.

The result of all this was that when these multinational corporations took over old-fashioned British undertakers, they brought with them the way they were used to doing things in France and America, where these things are regulated, and that upped the ante for everyone. Plus, as I said earlier, hygiene and health protocols are taken much more seriously since the arrival of AIDS.

Reasons to embalm

So, as I've said, unless you're having an open coffin funeral or the funeral's delayed, embalming is, given that undertakers today have refrigeration, illogical, un-ecofriendly and probably an unnecessary expense. But...

One step forward, two steps back

Big business's love of *Standardisation* had a beneficial effect when multinationals brought their way of doing things to embalming, but some other things that big business likes could have potentially less desirable effects.

Centralisation and *Economies of Scale* as practised by every big company from Tesco to Amazon could have a kind of knock-on effect that may paradoxically, given a certain set of circumstances, make embalming a good idea if you're dealing with one of the big funeral companies.

Just like smaller undertakers or family firms with a few shops in the same area, big companies do all the embalming in one place. The difference is, their regional embalming facilities serve more branches, which can sometimes be spread across a large area.

So some bodies might end up being driven a long way from somewhere on the edge of the regional catchment area to the central embalming and storage site. They may then have to be taken all the way back again to the local branch for viewing, and ultimately, cremation or burial.

The problem is, while the central site and the branches have refrigeration, the vans don't. And because of the larger catchment area, and the larger number of branches served, Centralisation and Economies of Scale mean that the vans have larger distances to travel, and more stops to make. So if it's hot weather, and there's some traffic congestion…

Unless you have an open coffin viewing or funeral, it would never cause problems anyway, and it all seems very hypothetical, but nevertheless, it is something I personally have known to happen, even if it was only once, and this is the only explanation.

VII

More 'Inconvenient Biochemistry' for the Undertaker

The petrochemical industry trick of flaring off unwanted gases (but via a trocar rather than an oil rig) is how the undertaker deals with one of the byproducts of death's chemistry, but there are others.

To explain what they are, I have to tell you what happens to a body from the moment of death onwards, and more specifically, about the biochemistry of rigor mortis and cellular decomposition.

Out of consideration for those of you with unhappy memories of physics and chemistry lessons, or whose eyes glaze over at the mention of this type of thing, I've done my best to make the language as untechnical as possible. You may find some compensation in the descriptions of how the real-life consequences are dealt with in practice.

Post Mortem changes

are, in order of appearance:

Primary *flaccidity*, or "going floppy", which happens at the moment of death, and affects the whole body UNLESS

Cadaveric spasm occurs, which also happens at the moment of death, and usually violent death, but is much less common in real life (or should that be real death?) than it seems to be in crime novels and TV cop shows. This is where your gun has to be pried from your cold dead hand if you're in the NRA, or where the detective (or 'sleuth') opens the victim's clenched hand to reveal a button from the murderer's coat.

Pallor mortis, or "going white", which happens almost immediately, very obviously in the case of people who are pale to begin with.

Algor Mortis is the loss of heat from the body, which continues until it's the same temperature as its surroundings.

Rigor mortis is caused the disappearance of a chemical called ATP from the body some time after death. The default setting for muscle fibres is 'contract', and their cells use energy to stop them doing that, and to alter their length when the muscle is used. Adenosine Tri-Phosphate is used to produce energy in cells, and it stops being made at the moment of death.

Afterwards, even though you're dead, this purely chemical process carries on until the stockpiles of ATP run out. It's rather odd to think that after electrical activity in the brain and nervous system has stopped, and the digestive juices have started eating the lining of the stomach and intestines and bacteria are at work, the chemical process that animated the body in a physical sense is still going on.

It usually takes 2-3 hours after death for the ATP to be used up, or maybe more if, for instance, the body's somewhere warm. As it disappears, rigor 'sets in' and the muscles become rigid.

It first shows in the eyelids. That's why people close the eyes just after someone's died – if you try to do it after rigor's set in, the eyelids won't close.

It then affects the face, and after that the neck and shoulders, and travels downwards from there. It stays for anything from three hours to three or four days, and then it disappears in the same order it appeared (resulting in *secondary flaccidity*).

How long this all takes is very variable, depending on age, build, physical fitness, if there'd been any illness or recent physical exercise, what temperature the body was exposed to, any wind chill etc.

It doesn't appear at all in babies or children, or, sometimes, and very rarely, in adults.

It's very awkward removing a body with rigor if it's in a confined space. The worst I had was a man in his late fifties who'd died on the lavatory. It was in some kind of hostel or halfway house for addicts or alcoholics, a big Victorian house that had been converted into individual rooms for inmates.

The toilet was three flights up a narrow staircase that was so steep and had such sharp turns that it was like a spiral staircase. It was in a kind of turret attached to the corner of the building. It was just a toilet, not a bathroom, and so small and narrow it was like a cupboard.

What you would normally do is put the body on its back, and gently waggle the limbs around and rub them until they became more pliable – you can forget all the stuff you've seen in films where they grab an arm and violently wrench it so it suddenly gives way with a loud crack like a tree branch snapping.

The problem was, there was nowhere to lie him down. He'd died slumped to one side against the wall, with his elbows on his knees. It was difficult enough to get the door open, never mind get him out.

We had to prop the stretcher up at an angle with the head end against the wall next to the toilet and the foot jammed against the skirting board opposite, then lift him out and strap him onto it, like a statue of Rodin's Thinker, and attach the stretcher cover (which was too narrow) over him as best we could. He was only wearing his Y fronts, so, as so often happens, death was undignified, with an element of farce.

Livor mortis is the pooling of blood in the body caused by gravity. The iron in the red corpuscles makes them heavy, so they sink through the capillaries and settle. The areas lowest down end up looking bruised and purplish-red. It doesn't appear where the flesh is pinched or compressed between the body and the surface it's resting on, so the underside regions show a kind of high-contrast contour marking.

It starts just after death, and takes four or five hours. After that the corpuscles congeal and the marking is fixed. It gets darker and darker for some hours, then gradually disappears as the body decomposes.

As we all know from TV and detective stories, if the lividity isn't where it should be, the body's been moved after death.

Decomposition ("getting an inflated reputation")
Decomposition is the break-down of the body. The first outward signs are caused by bacteria in the gut, and appear as a greenish tinge and bloating in the upper abdomen, which I've already covered under embalming, and I've also mentioned the fact that as soon as aerobic bacteria have used up the oxygen in the tissues, *an*aerobic bacteria multiply and produce gases like methane and hydrogen sulphide. This is the first stage of decomposition, and it's called *Putrefaction,* but there is another process, slower-acting, but set in motion at the moment of death just the same.

That is *Autolysis*, which is Greek for 'self destruction'. Enzymes in living cells break down chemicals to make things the cells need. They are kept in check in living cells by other chemical processes which protect the structure of the cell and the cell wall.

After death, the walls dissolve and the cell contents can be got at by any bacteria that happen to be on the other side of the cell wall. Apart from the gut, the greatest concentrations of bacteria are in the throat and nose, and the genitals, where it also so happens that the tissues are only protected by thin mucous membranes which no longer have a working immune system to keep the bacteria out.

The gas that these bacteria produce makes the lips, tongue and soft palate swell until the tongue protrudes. On the outside it looks like a big fat sandwich made from three pieces of calf's tongue off the butcher's slab has been jammed in the mouth.
And the balls and scrotum swell up to the size of a jaffa orange, or even a pomelo.

Autolysis is what makes rigor mortis wear off – the connections between muscle fibres break, and the muscles can stretch again. Embalming works by killing bacteria, but it also removes the enzymes that cause autolysis, so the body 'sets' in the position it was in when it was embalmed – unlike rigor, this doesn't wear off until bacterial decomposition weakens the connections between the fibres.

"Losing one's grip"

The outer layer of skin, being dead, is unaffected by autolysis, but the layer attaching it to the cells underneath is attacked by enzymes leaking from the cells, and soon separates. This has the effect of loosening the skin, which can then easily tear, and of producing a slimy vaseline-like slick on the underside.

The end result can be a very unpleasant surprise when you try to move a body in this condition. The standard technique involves two people, one at either end. The stretcher is placed next to the body, one person grasps the hands, the other the ankles, and both lift in unison to raise the body and place it on the stretcher.

If you try that with a body in this state (and there might be no obvious external signs), the one at the head end finds that as he lifts, the skin on the hands slips straight off, leaving him holding a pair of greasy human-skin gloves.

VIII

Back to Balmer's...

One thing about Balmer's that has puzzled me ever since was the time Dave was handed a black bin bag by Maurice on the way out of Thrale's (the shop with the back room where the embalming took place). I asked him what it was, and he said it was to go to the crematorium. When I asked him what was in it, he said it was leftovers from the embalming. When I asked how there could be "leftovers", he just shrugged. I got the impression this was a regular event, like taking cast-off clothes to Oxfam.

It went in the downstairs section of the hearse, behind the black leatherette flap that hung over the entrance to the underfloor storage, and when we got to the crematorium, sure enough, after we'd handed in the paperwork for that week's cremations at the office at the front gate, we parked round the back of the crematorium itself and went in the back way to where we normally popped downstairs for (appropriately enough) a smoke while the service was on.

That was only if you were driving a limo, when you had to wait for the mourners, of course – the hearse would be off at a fair old pace as soon as they'd all gone in the chapel. The idea was that if you left the back lid up and wound the windows down, a bit of speed had the effect of blowing away the petals and leaves that had fallen from the floral tributes, saving you the job of crawling into the back to sweep it out – a labour-saving tip Dave proudly demonstrated when I first started.

The hearse usually got driven pretty fast between jobs as well, in the same way most drivers floor it at the first bit of open road after a traffic jam, and being a top-end model with a big engine but much lighter bodywork, it had a bit of zip – and there's no chance of being done for speeding.

Dave told me that the police never stop hearses or undertaker's vans, and so it proved in practice. This was a perk of the job that Dave exploited in full, as I will explain later.

Being a top-end model it also had a top-end sound system with powerful speakers. We used to like driving slowly along busy streets belting out Jimmy Hendrix or something similarly incongruous so loud that the windows bulged in and out in sympathy, watching people craning round to see where it was coming from.

Dave also told me that hearses are the only vehicles on the road apart from the Queen's that don't need a tax disc:

> "It's from the days when they were all horsedrawn."

It was true Balmer's hearse didn't have a tax disc at the time, but I think that said more about Balmer's than it did about the rules of the road, because I noticed their competitors had tax discs. Horsedrawn hearses aren't taxed, but that's because they're horsedrawn.

But back to the black bag. Dave handed it over to the assistant manager, and it disappeared into a back room with nothing said on either part.

I believe Dave's uncharacteristic coyness was a wind-up, and he was saying nothing simply because it amused him to get my imagination working overtime thinking of gruesome possibilities. When I asked him again after we got back in the hearse, he just smiled mysteriously.

I discovered later that there is an embalmer's etiquette, and that stuffing blood and body fluid-stained surgical wipes and gloves into the last body of the day before sewing it up, as some did in those days, was frowned on by the better kind of embalmer. I imagine there might also have been a chance of some bad PR if a cat scratched open a black bag full of that kind of stuff while it was waiting for the binmen on the pavement outside your discreet and dignified local family undertakers.

Incinerating it at the crematorium between jobs would be a good solution to the problem.

Upright and Manly Bearing, Grave Demeanour

Being tall and upright is normally desirable for bearers. There used to be a tradition of using ex-servicemen for casual bearing, when there's a couple of funerals on at the same time and not enough full-timers. You used to be able to spot casuals in pubs near funeral shops or cemeteries – they'd be the ones drinking their cash in hand plus share of the tips wearing a black overcoat with a coffin-edge shaped dent in one shoulder.

Speaking of tips, you're usually told they're 'for a drink' when they're offered. Balmer's official policy was not to accept them, which meant if one of the Balmers was watching, you had to do that. Otherwise, they were gratefully accepted.

The traditional response on being offered a tip is

> "Best respects.", with a nod of the head or tip of the hat.

And speaking of funeral drinks (traditionally whisky), I know of one crematorium with a drinks licence – I always thought they should open a nightclub there called 'Ashes'.

Apart from an upright and manly bearing (caused by a deformed back – my lumbar and sacral vertebrae are fused together, giving the effect of a scaffolding pole shoved up my arse), I personally have another natural characteristic that might be considered a plus in the funeral business. A stone face. As if I'd been using botox before it was invented. (Interesting how quickly people started pronouncing it 'boat-ox', almost as if were from the rhyming slang 'boat race', for face. Can anyone really pronounce botulism with a long 'o'?)

Where I come from, showing emotion is unmanly, and you also learn at an early age to keep a poker face to avoid giving anyone the chance to say "What're you smilin' at?" as a pretext for violence.

Also, never glancing in the general direction of male faces, to foil the ceaseless vigilance for the chance to use the other favourite:

> "Oo're you lookin' at?"

I suspect that's why I got the job, and as for being tall, unlike everyone else there when I started, I think it was because Maurice's supposedly retired dad sat in on the interview (which I later discovered was unusual – perhaps it was because I was from the Labour Exchange, which, as I've already said, was also unusual). He probably subscribed to the ex-servicemen-casual-bearer-tradition and liked my 'military' bearing.

Concentration of Camp

Maurice, the boss at Balmer's, was gay, which is not unusual in the funeral business. I suppose it's not necessarily unusual in any business, just that perhaps in some businesses people tend to keep quiet about it. Football and boxing, for instance.

For some reason, gay funeral directors weren't uncommon then (and not just at Balmer's), nor do they seem to be now. I don't know why this might be (or perhaps the funeral business is just one of the ones where people don't feel they need to keep it quiet?), but at the risk of sounding glib, and reinforcing stereotypes, perhaps the reasons might be similar to the ones you hear for gay priests: more empathy than straight men, less emotionally repressed, hence better at expressing sympathy, together with a generally more developed interest in fashion and style.
Pacing in front of a hearse in a Victorian outfit with a top hat on and swinging a silver-topped cane certainly ticks the box on the style front.

Funeral director is the job title for shop managers. They deal with the public and handle the cash. The pay is poor compared to middle management in service industries generally, just as it is for the chauffeur bearers and clerical staff in undertaking.

A flat above the business, usually a pretty large one, used to be a perk of the job that went some way to making up for the poor wages, but not so much these days – since the business only needs the ground floor for the office and a chapel of rest for viewing bodies, and rents being what they are, the tendency is to let the flat above and get the going rate.

The gay funeral directors I knew mostly seemed to adopt a US forces-style 'don't ask, don't tell' approach, but there was a certain elevated level of campness when the public weren't around.

"Eyes like a Japanese welder"

I suspect the general prevalence of shortness at Balmer's came from the fact that Maurice normally did the hiring and firing, and he was.

In his early forties, dark-haired, thinning on top with a very low side-parting, chubby, and with a permanently narrowed gaze through specs with big lenses – as if he was playing poker, and trying to tell if you were bluffing. Or like a suspicious and rather severe Dennis Taylor – the snooker player that had the big specs that worked upside down.

What that means, for those of you not interested in snooker (which actually includes me, but I have, as you may have gathered by now, a 'fly-paper mind'), is that he had big eighties-style specs with the side-pieces meeting the frames at the bottom, so when he was down at the table sighting along his cue, he was looking through his specs, not over the top of them.

Perks of the job

I didn't get on the rota to be on call for quite a while after I'd started, because I always tried to avoid it, and everyone else was so eager to do it. The extra money that they were all so keen on didn't seem worth it for the inconvenience of being dragged out of your bed to drive to the other side of town in the middle of the night to do a removal, especially since there was nothing to stop the same thing happening more than once in one night, or every night on the trot while you were down for it.

Neither was having the use of the van much of a draw for me, although there was a kind of downmarket Hammer Horror glamour in having to be in uniform if you went out, and in standing up and announcing that you had to go and shift a dead body to a morgue if you got the call when you were at a dinner party (not to mention turning up in an undertaker's van).

I always wore a black suit with a waistcoat on those occasions, rather than the shiny grey polyester rubbish that Balmer's had given me – I thought of that as more like overalls.

Just to explain "removals": on my first day, as we were walking to the van after I'd changed into my uniform, Dave asked if I'd done removals before?

I thought it was some kind of question to judge my lifting ability, and started telling him about the time I had to get an office safe down a stairwell that was so narrow only two of us could get hold of it (the other unlucky bastard briefly became Pete Docherty's manager some years later), but that wasn't what he meant.

> "No: removals. Removal of the remains. Collecting bodies."

I'd just told Maurice in my interview that I'd been a casual for a big firm in another town years ago, but never driven. I told Dave the truth, that my brother had been a chauffeur bearer for the same firm, and his father-in-law a french polisher, but all I'd done was go out with him in the car for the ride a few times.

> "Well you'll be doing a lot of removals on this job. It's not bad – no-one knows where you are when you're out, and sometimes you get tips. But don't let those cunts in there know,"

jerking his thumb behind him at the building we'd just left,

> "they'll take them off you."

As I've already said, he was right about that, and just like other badly-paid workers, you needed tips to make up your wages to a living wage. That was why everyone else was so keen to be on call with the van.

That meant that you took the van home for 3, 4, or at most 5 nights, and if someone died and Balmer's got the job, you had to meet the shop manager for that area at the address, collect the body, and take it back to the shop, or more usually the morgue, which might not be the nearest morgue – it depends on which health authority the address comes under (anyone who dies without a doctor "in recent attendance" has to go to a morgue to be post-mortemed).

IX

PMs Question Time

More specifically, a post mortem is required by law if someone hasn't seen a doctor in the past two weeks or if there are "unusual circumstances". The preferred term in the US, and familiar to us from the never-ending stream of detective-based – or more correctly, detection-based – fiction in TV, films and books which stems from the US, is autopsy, which is Latin for "see for yourself".

With regard to this current, and beginning to seem historical, fad for whodunit-based fiction that never seems to show any signs of reaching an end, and which has moved from 'police procedural' to 'trauma and autopsy procedural' (not so much 'whodunit' as 'howdunit-in-all-the grisly-detail'): take heart, this has happened before, in the 1920s, and it came to an end then, although it took a good twenty years.

Think of Agatha Christie, Raymond Chandler, Edgar Wallace.

Although, come to think of it, maybe the whodunits were just temporarily eclipsed by war stories and then cold war spy stories, and now they've resumed their former dominance?

Playtex Cross Your Heart

In a post mortem, all the soft bits of the body get taken out for a once-over and then put back again, but not necessarily where they came from.

Most of it gets done by the morgue technicians, with the pathologist only doing the actual 'lift and separate' and scrutiny. As in the embalming suite, the body lies on its back on a stainless-steel or ceramic surface like a door-sized sink drainer, with grooves and a plug hole. The head is supported by a rubber neckrest like a bisected diabolo.
If it's a forensic post mortem, first of all the body gets a very thorough, all over, close-up inspection, and samples are taken from under the fingernails, from the orifices, etc, etc, as we know so well from TV cop shows.

After that, or to start with if it's a regular PM, the brain and internal organs are removed. Three cuts are made on the torso: two from the hollows under where the collar bones meet the shoulders, and one from the breastbone to the groin, meeting at a mid-point level with the armpits to make a Y-shaped hole. The ribs and sternum are opened up with shears. The organs are removed and put in bowls.

To remove the brain, a cut is made behind the ears and across the back of the head in the hair, where it won't show afterwards. The scalp is then peeled forward and laid over the face, and a bone cutter like a big version of the Dremmel rotary saw that model makers use takes the top of the skull off, just above the eyebrow line. The noise is like a really loud dentist's drill.

Then the brain is taken out, checked over, and weighed, along with the other organs.

The organs then go into a plastic bag (all of them, brain included) which then goes in the body cavity, after which the bodywall and scalp incisions are sewn back up so that nothing will show when the body's dressed and put in a coffin.

Virtual Post Mortems

This may all be a thing of the past in the very near future. Already in the case of babies and children, the post-mortem MRI (Magnetic Resonance Imaging), also known as MIA: Minimally Invasive Autopsy, is already as good as the regular type.

But, to return to out of hours collection of bodies…

Surprise, surprise

One call-out brought home something which I hadn't previously really thought about, something so shockingly obvious you don't need to waste any time thinking about because it's so self-evident, but which, when you are brought up against it, really is both shocking and obvious.

It was this: the dead bodies that we spent so much time in such unthinking close proximity to, that we felt the weight of, that we handled as what was in effect the stock in trade of our working day WERE ONCE ALIVE JUST LIKE US.

I know it looks stupid spelt out like that, and you'll be thinking, yes, that is self-evident, and it's hardly any kind of profound philosophical statement; but unless you're a doctor or a nurse or a soldier, it's very likely that your appreciation of that fact is on an unsuspectedly superficial level.

Let me explain: I was woken up at about two in the morning and told to go to an address in an area of two-storey Victorian terraces, originally built as artisan housing and now an uneasy mixture of remnant working class occupants and middle classes on the first rung of the housing ladder.

You can tell who's who in these circumstances from the front gardens:

Privet hedge, tiny patch of lawn with borders/optional flagstones
= Original white working class (now pensioners);

Hugely overgrown/hacked to within an inch of its life hedge, car/motorbike parts, old furniture/white goods/empty fishtanks
= Incomers from periods preceding property boom, that is to say white working class or immigrants;

No hedge/garden, gravel/flagstones with box/laurel/treefern in centre
= Young 'professional' couple (the clincher here is a front door lacquered to a gleaming finish in a dark or primary colour with brass fittings designed for a grander and more imposing door).

This house had a neatly-trimmed privet hedge and picket fence. I was meeting Maurice there. That wasn't always the case, sometimes you picked up the shop manager on the way.

When I got there, I spotted his car and double parked with the back of the van lined up with the front door of the house for easy access, then settled down to wait until he came out and gave me the nod – he would have condoling and form-proffering to do before we moved the body.

It was a chilly night with the stars clearly visible between fast-moving clouds, and a half moon, with the street and pavements gleaming from some drizzle earlier in the evening.

When Maurice appeared at the front door I went round the back of the van and collected the stretcher, then went in as he held the door open and closed it quietly behind me. This house, its doll's house proportions, layout, furnishings, faded wallpaper and ingrained scent of meat & two veg was familiar to me from the houses of mine and my friend's grandparents in my childhood.

The hall and stair lights were unusually dim, with 40 watt bulbs and dark fabric shades. The house was silent, with light coming from under the front parlour door next to my left shoulder. I was very conscious of the family? wife? husband? son? listening to us on the other side of it.

"It's upstairs," Maurice whispered "folllow me."

Etiquette on these occasions requires that the removal is done as discreetly as possible, with the family kept out of the way. This is because you may have to manhandle a stretcher with an awkward load strapped to it vertically or sideways on over banisters and round tight corners on the stairs or landings.

Although perhaps there's more to it than that. On my first day in the job, removing a body from a nursing home, Dave insisted that the nurse leave the room before we started, and then impressed on me with a seriousness that was unusual for him that you must never, ever allow anyone else to be present on these occasions (more of that later).

At the top of the stairs on the left was a box-like bedroom whose window, now with tightly-drawn curtains, would have looked down on the back yard and pent-roofed outside toilet extension, probably now used as a tool shed.

The room was unhealthily hot, feverishly hot, and dimly lit by a bedside lamp whose light was strangled by a wire-framed fabric shade with bobbles on. Coming from outdoors in my suit and gabardine mac it felt like the tropical greenhouse in a botanic gardens.

A single bed was directly under the window, with the head end butted up against the wall and the space between the foot and the other wall neatly filled with a narrow wardrobe.

> "The doctor's just left. Put the stretcher on the bed and we'll roll him onto it."

The bed was piled high with brushed nylon sheets, blankets, an eiderdown and (something I hadn't seen since my childhood) a candlewick bedspread.

In it was an obese, dark-haired man in his forties with a liver-coloured face frowning slightly and with an expression of concentrating with his eyes closed; revealed as Maurice threw the bedclothes back.

He was wearing dark-coloured polyester pyjamas with the jacket and pants unfastened, and sagged into the loosely-sprung mattress as if it were a hammock.

I slipped the needlecord cover off the stretcher, then attempted to lay the stretcher on the bed, but there wasn't room.

"Put it on the floor. You take his legs." hissed Maurice.

I laid the stretcher on the floor, part under the bed because there was so little room, and we stood side by side and got hold of him.

At the first touch, I felt almost as physically startled as if I'd just been given an electric shock or a slap in the face. He was warm – and not just room temperature, but hot, as if he'd just stepped out of a hot bath.

For the first time in the job, I had a physical, visceral understanding that this had actually been a living person just like me, and for the first time in my life I realised as an incontrovertible physical fact that I was going to die.

It really was an intense and personal *revelation*, in the original, unsullied by repetition and cliché, sense of the word.

After that moment of philosophical profundity, the farcical juxtaposition of events so often found in real life took over.

We had to lean over him, and I had to put one arm under his legs and get hold of him at the same time as Maurice, but he was so heavy that we were forced to roll him rather than lift him, and after being poised in precarious equilibrium on the edge of the bed, the tired mattress suddenly gave way and we found ourselves unable to prevent his sudden descent onto the waiting stretcher with a thud that shook the room, and probably the whole house.

Getting him out of the room was bad enough, but manoeuvring the absurdly overburdened stretcher over the banisters and down the stairs was almost beyond us.

I was at the bottom, at the foot end, because I was bigger, and at one point I found my legs and arms trembling with the strain so much that I felt sure I was going to either fold up onto my knees with the stretcher crushing me so I couldn't get up, or lose my grip and have the bloody thing go surfing down the stairs.

When we arrived at the foot of the stairs there wouldn't have been room to lay him down and get the front door open as well, so Maurice laid down his end on one of the stairs and I held my end up at waist height while Maurice squeezed past to get the front door open, then returned to take up his place at the top end again, and we made our way out of the house.

As I passed the parlour door, I imagined the man's mother sitting on the other side, listening to all our panting and wrestling with her son's corpse on the stairs in the deathly silent house – not to mention the crash landing when he rolled off the bed.

X

Sex & Death and Art & Law

The possibly higher than average incidence of gayness amongst funeral directors seems, in my experience, to have escaped the prurient attention of the general public, perhaps because that attention seems to be so well focused on one prurient subject in particular.

There seems to be a well-established branch of the urban myth or factoid bank of apocryphal knowledge that everyone draws on that leads them to 'know' of some kind of fourth or fifth-hand tale of an undertaker's employee or morgue attendant being caught on the job with a stiff.

A bit like everyone seems to know of someone whose eye has come out of its socket (an industrial accident, or during surgery under local anaesthetic, etc) 'so that they could see their own cheek' before it was put back. Or maybe this is a working class thing? Not talking of an eye being like a button on a bit of dangling thread, but 'knowing' stories like this. But surely everyone tells each other stories like this when they're at school?

Anyway, it's rubbish. An eye isn't on a bit of elastic, once it comes out it stays out. And it doesn't come out very easily either; aside from the fact that the optic nerve isn't elastic, there are muscles attached all round the edges.

And I've never heard any stories of necrophiliac funeral or hospital staff.

People dying on the job, I've heard of – reaching orgasm... like running for a bus... strain on the heart etc – but the only Sex & Death story I can do is that the best pair of tits I've ever seen were on a dead woman in her 60s – no, that trivialises it – the *finest pair of breasts* I've ever seen.

It was a removal from a posh house on a fringe of Balmer's territory that bordered on an upmarket area.

The first surprise was being led into a room on the ground floor, immediately after walking through the front door, that wasn't made up as a bedroom – most people who die at home die in bed, or on the toilet (straining at stool... unaccustomed exertion... weak heart etc again).

The second was that the body was laid out on a big sideboard against the wall, like a buffet from a Peter Greenaway film. Laying out is rare nowadays even in working class homes with rural Irish connections, and this was a middle class home, and the name on the jobsheet was English. And in a laying out, the body's normally in a coffin on trestles in the middle of the room.

The body was draped with a sheet, and underneath it more surprises: the eyes were open, and the body was dressed in nothing but a pair of white panties. But the most remarkable thing of all was the sculptural perfection of the physique, like something carved in alabaster; most notably a pair of breasts of quite exceptional pert- and upstanding-ness.

Believe me, they would have been exceptional for any woman of any age lying on her back, but particularly, outrageously, in the case of one who was dead and in her mid sixties. Not large, but with absolutely no sag, and a perfect double-curvature, ogee profile like the cupolas of the Taj Mahal, and beautifully proportioned nipples. And before you ask, yes, they were real, there were no scars where any silicone bags had gone in.

It may be that she'd asked to be laid out like this in her will. Or it may have been something she specifically prohibited. It wouldn't have made any difference legally – that being a matter of a dead body not belonging to anyone, or as they put it in the legal profession: no property in a corpse.

(No) Man's Estate/Vacant Possession

That's why, regardless of what you say in your will, even if you were a life-long opponent of cremation, if your relatives decide they want you cremated, that's what happens.

Or in other words:

> "The deceased did not own their body and could not bequeath it to their estate. The estate can claim the body for decent disposal, although not necessarily as the deceased would have wished."
> Margaret Brazier, *Retained Organs: Ethics and Humanity*, Oxford Journal of Legal Studies, 2002.

If you want to look it up, the legal precedent goes: R v. Sharpe, 1857, Doodeward v. Spence, 1908 and R v. Kelly, 1998.

The first one was about the Church of England's rights over consecrated ground (a son moved his mother's body to a Catholic cemetery and the church charged him with theft of a body), but part of the judgement was "Our law recognises no property in a corpse".

The second was a case in Australia in which a doctor had preserved a two-headed stillborn baby that he'd kept after he delivered it.

The law got involved when it was sold off after he died. It was exhibited in a freak show, and in the court case that followed it's being seized by the police, the judge ruled that although there was no property in a corpse, "application of skill", for instance in making a mummy or a medical specimen, means that it becomes different from a corpse, and is capable of becoming property.

So, ok then, it makes sense that the plastinated bodies that Dr von Hagens exhibits should belong to him, but all that the two-headed baby doctor did was stick it in a bottle and pickle it. There's certainly more "application of skill" in embalming – so does that mean that an embalmed body becomes the undertaker's property in law?

The third legal precedent, strangely enough, brings us to the area of Death & Art.

Regina versus Kelly, Regina versus Lindsay, to give it its full title, was a case in which an artist (Anthony Noel Kelly) had exhibited casts of human body parts used in the preparation of medical specimens at the Royal College of Surgeons in London.

Kelly was a drawing tutor at the Prince of Wales' School of Architecture and he'd been going to the Royal

College of Surgeons to make sketches of medical specimens for illustrations.

He liked the look of the specimens so much he tried modelling them in clay from his sketches, but he didn't like the look of his sculpture as much as he liked the look of the real thing, so he got a trainee lab technician (who, curiously enough, had previously worked as an embalmer) to smuggle bits out in bin bags for him.

He kept them in his studio while he made casts of them, and afterwards he took them to his family home where he gave them a 'decent burial'.

As you do.

All this sounds very odd, and what sounds even odder is that it seems he hadn't really taken in that what he was doing might be considered wrong, but you might begin to realise how if you knew he'd always been fascinated with bits of dead bodies.

Before he was sketching medical specimens, previous employment included working in an abattoir and a butcher's, and an earlier art project involved DIY embalming of horses' legs.

Oh, and the family home where he laid the human heads, limbs and bits of torsos to rest was a castle in Kent, and his uncle's the Duke of Norfolk.

It seems he thought that what he was doing was ok because he'd been told the Royal College of Surgeons were only meant to use these donated bodies for three years, after which they were supposed to be buried; and these bits were all past their sell-by date.

I don't think the Royal College of Surgeons would have been burying them in someone's back garden though, even if it was the garden of a stately home, and a man of the cloth and some ceremony probably would have been involved.

Show(n) into the drawing room

He then made plaster casts of limbs and torsos, sprayed them with silver paint, and hung them on the wall at the Contemporary Art Fair in 1997.

The Contemporary Art Fair doesn't exist now, but at the time it was a big event in the London art world calendar where galleries hired stands in the Business Design Centre in Islington (which must have felt like a home from home, given Kelly's employment history – it used to be the Royal Agricultural Hall, where cattle were sold for slaughter). Kelly's work was shown by Jibby Beane, a former model who started out as an art dealer by showing friends' work in her front room.

The police got involved because Her Majesty's Inspector of Anatomy (which sound like someone who vets top-shelf magazines for Buckingham Palace) made his own investigation after reading about the exhibition in a newspaper and working out from the photos that the artworks must have been made from casts of actual body parts. He then wrote to everywhere that kept bodies for medical instruction asking them to check their records to see if any parts were missing.

A very ticklish business, I'm sure – to put it in "a police spokesman"-style jargon, they had to "make enquiries", because their "attention had been drawn to the matter", but "given the sensitive nature of the allegations", and "the undesirability of publicity" for, first and foremost, relatives or friends of the donors of the body parts, or indeed anyone who had donated their bodies to science at the Royal College of Surgeons, and, second, the effect such publicity might have on the future of the donation programme and the reputation of the Royal College of Surgeons, and also given the uncertainties of any prosecution succeeding, the law concerning property of a dead body being what it is – they would probably want any enquiries they did make to be "discreet".

Kelly owned up and went to court, though, where he was convicted under the Theft Act 1968. He was sentenced to nine months, with no bail. His partner in what now was, for the first time in British legal history, a crime, got off with six months suspended.

This set legal precedent because, although plenty of 'resurrectionists' were sent to jail in the 18th century for digging up bodies and selling them for dissection, it was for "outraging public decency'" not theft of human remains.

On appeal, the convictions were upheld because although:

> "…it has now been the common law for 150 years that neither a corpse nor parts of a corpse are in themselves and without more capable of being property protected by rights: see, for example, Erle J. delivering the judgement of a powerful Court for Crown Cases reserved in *Regina v. Sharpe* (1857) where he said: 'Our law recognises no property in a corpse…'".

and to change that would require an Act of Parliament,

"...parts of a corpse are capable of being property within section 4 of the Theft Act 1968 if they have acquired different attributes by virtue of the application of skill, such as dissection or preservation techniques, for exhibition or teaching purposes...".

Lord Justice Rose, Vice President, Court of Appeal (Criminal Division), May 1998.

Lord Justice Rose went on to say that common law didn't stand still, and that if the question arose on some future occasion, courts would hold that body parts were capable of being property even "without the acquisition of different attributes" – such as being turned into medical specimens – "if they had a use or significance beyond their mere existence" as organ transplants, or for DNA extraction, for instance.

But that still wouldn't apply to dead bodies in ordinary circumstances, so what happens to yours will still depend on what your relatives or executors decide, not what you tell them or write in your will (and US law being close enough in this respect, it's the same in most states there).

Final rinse

Over time, medical specimens like those kept at the Royal College of Surgeons become more and more unrecognisable in appearance and texture – shrunken, dried-out and stiff – and their dissection could become less like a means to absorb real-life principles of human anatomy in preparation for surgery, and more like part of an apprenticeship for shoemaking or saddlery.

In at least one teaching hospital I know, technicians like Anthony Noel's mate get round the problem by an imaginative new application of a well-known household product almost certainly undreamt of by its manufacturers.

The day before bodies or body parts are needed – it might be twenty or so heads to be set out bright and early the next morning in rows on desks ready for future brain surgeons to get to grips with – they are removed from their formaldehyde baths (or buckets, or Tupperware containers) and placed in a new bath of a weaker solution with a few spoonfuls of the aforementioned well-known household product.

Overnight, the misbegotten, tough-as-old-boots specimens fill out and regain all their original softness and delicacy of texture, like flowers in the rain.

And the miracle ingredient?

The loving touch of new Lenor.

You probably wouldn't want to rub your cheek up against those fibres like a cat looking for a feed, the way young women in adverts do with the nap on their newly-washed angora sweaters, but this familiar domestic product does just as good a job in the anatomy lab as it does in the laundry room – and in this case, the peculiar artificial pungency that fabric conditioners are 'fragranced' with might actually be a bonus.

XI

Underworld Undertakers

I guessed there was more to Dave than met the eye on my very first day at Balmer's when I was paired with him for him to instruct me in the duties of a chauffeur bearer. We were putting floral tributes on the top of the hearse – MAM, NAN, DAD and the like.

They get put on the pavement outside the shop for the mourners to look at when they assemble for the cortege, then the big ones go on top of the hearse and the smaller ones go inside with the cellophane-wrapped bouquets, with more of those in the boots of the limos, too, if there's a lot of them.

Then when you get to the crematorium, they get laid out outside, along with all the ones for the other cremations that morning or afternoon, in order of appearance (or rather, disappearance). Or round the grave if it's a burial.

You use florist's wire to attach them to the rails on the hearse roof; thin ductile iron, soft enough to cut, but stiff enough to hold its shape.

I'd started bending the wire from side to side to get it to break from metal fatigue when Dave said

"'Ere y'are, look out, I'll do that."

I was a bit surprised when my new workmate produced a giant Opinel lock-knife that was a good ten inches long when he opened it out. I must have looked surprised, but all he did was give me a sunny smile and slice through the wire.

Dave was short (of course, like everyone else at Balmer's), round-shouldered and smiled a lot. Think of a cheeky working-class British version of Napoleon with lots of charm.

He was easy to talk to, and I soon felt as if I'd known him for a long time. He liked to take the piss, and often got away with remarks to Maurice or the shop bosses that no-one else would, usually delivered in the kind of undertone that was perfectly audible to everyone, but not quite so loud that the object of the remark would be forced to acknowledge they'd heard it.

He liked to flout instruction he saw as unnecessary whenever possible, and the act of giving an order often seemed to provoke an immediate and contrary reaction which would have been absent if no order had been given.

When, for instance, in my first week in the job, Simon, a flamboyantly gay funeral director who Dave always referred to as "Gaylord", told us to wait outside the church because the funeral service would probably be short (the coffin was staying on the hearse, so we weren't needed for bearing), the minute he'd gone inside, Dave said:

> "Fuck this, I'm going for a cup of tea – you comin'?"

The church was in the middle of what must have been a kind of village green a long time in the past, with shops round it, and we went over to a pastry shop for take-away pasties and tea in polystyrene cups. (For American readers, in Britain 'pasties' are a kind of savoury pastry, not something used by burlesque artistes.)

Dave must have known there wasn't really time, because he started walking back to the church at a brisk pace as soon as we'd got them, eating as he went.

Before we were half way there, Simon appeared from the porch entrance ahead of the congregation, and we had to race across to the cars stuffing boiling hot pasty into our gobs and casting cups and greaseproof paper aside as we went.

Simon glared at us both as we held the car doors open for the mourners, while wiping our mouths with the backs of our hands.

Dave's comment (and his favourite catchphrase):

"Fuck 'em if they can't take a joke."

I mentioned earlier that hearses don't seem to get stopped for speeding, and the fact that undertakers seemed to be off the radar for police was something that Dave took advantage of. It seemed he supplemented the poor wages that Balmer's paid through some kind of shady parallel activity.

As long as you turned up where you were wanted, and collected and delivered as and when necessary, Balmer's weren't bothered what you did inbetween, or where exactly you were.

I noticed we often took strange detours on our way to the morgue or a shop as it might be, through housing estates or streets that didn't seem to be on our way, and that these digressions involved Dave paying brief doorstep visits to "just do a bit of business". I don't know what he was up to, whether he was some kind of freelance Freeman's agent, or what, and I didn't ask.

I also discovered in due course that he had a council flat that he didn't live in, but where he kept two Doberman Pinschers, as we made daily meat deliveries on their behalf while on our rounds – the door would be opened, the meat flung in, and the door shut, smartly, before the dogs could get you.

He was originally curious to know if I'd ever been a copper, and, having made frequent comments about my looking like one, in time came to accept that I hadn't, although he always kept looking for signs of law-abiding tendencies in me – he would for instance throw his chip paper or empty fag packet out of the van window and then say:

"You don't like that, do yer?"

Our boss, Maurice, often used to make pointed comments about Dave not being "away" at Christmas and letting him down like he did last year. When I eventually asked what this was about, I discovered that Dave had spent the last Christmas period in prison, on remand for headbutting his pregnant girlfriend,

"…but it was all her own fault, Bob. She wound me up until I couldn't help myself. She did it to get back at me for something I'd done."

As I've said though, he had a good sense of humour and loads of charm, was very good with the families, and took the important parts of the job very seriously.

Although, of course, I never wound him up until he couldn't help himself, to get back at him for something he'd done.

On my first day we did a removal from an old people's home. We had to collect a granny who was lying under a sheet on top of her bed. The nurse that showed us the way wanted to help, and when Dave said

"No thanks, we can manage.",

she said very briskly, but in a good-humoured way

"Don't be silly, I do this all the time.",

as if he was suffering from an excess of manly pride, and attempted to carry on.

Dave was serious to start with, but now he became positively stern, and repeated WITH EMPHASIS

"NO THANKS, WE CAN MANAGE."

After she'd left, he shut the door firmly and said

"You never let anyone stay in the room when you're doin' this."

The point being that it's undignified, and the fewer people that see it the better, out of respect for the deceased.

Dave told me an interesting story about the assistant manager of one of the crematoriums.

If I wanted any hard porn, he was the man to see. Apparently he smuggled it in in air trays. Yes, 'trays':

that's what they call boxes for shipping bodies by air, for some reason. They're made in America, and the best ones are Ziegler transfer cases, originally made for transporting Jewish bodies, which, being unembalmed, mean that the case has to be a giant biohazard container.

So you see, these international airline caskets are hermetically sealed metal shells, and Customs (sorry, the "Border Protection Agency" as it is now)

> "never open them because anyone who ever has opened one never does it again: the smell stinks the whole airport out".

Drugs, too, apparently. But this must be a funeral trade urban myth – surely Customs would just open the casket outdoors if they wanted to open it?

Bad Venn

People in the trade now find these stories as incredible as I did at the time, and I'm told that no-one would get away with that type of thing today, and I have no reason to doubt that; but I would also point to the fact that Dave had mates in other local firms who he did business with, and he would often stop in traffic for a chinwag when we came across them, and there was much serious talking out of the side of the mouth and making of sidelong glances when they met at crematoria.

How much this had to do with me catching a glimpse of a tenuous network connecting isolated individuals who were in a tiny bad-apple minority, and how much it might have had to do with Balmer's having lax standards of employment is anybody's guess, but just keeping abreast of general news reveals at least some overlap between the criminal and undertaking worlds still exists today.

Partial observance of the Unwritten Law

For instance, when Norwegian customs officials broke the rule that hearses never get stopped, and pulled over a Latvian hearse at the border with Sweden in September 2013, they found 473 litres of alcohol and 20,000 cigarettes inside the aluminium case in the back rather than the dead Norwegian that was supposed to be in there.

They'd stopped the hearse in the first place because large amounts of contraband were being seized on the way in from Latvia at the time.

But even though a suspiciously nervous driver and dodgy paperwork gave them every right to, respect for the unwritten law meant they still didn't open the casket until it had been through an x-ray machine.

Nonagenarian Cancerous Bone Marrow from America

After Alistair Cooke died of cancer, it was discovered that samples of his bone marrow had been supplied to cancer clinics for transplant treatment of cancer patients as part of a widespread scam perpetrated by criminal funeral directors.

If you're too young to remember him, and think perhaps he might play cricket for England, he was a much-loved Brit journalist who'd lived in America since before the Second World War and made radio broadcasts home called *Letter from America* that everyone listened to. And I mean everyone: the BBC World Service put them out round the world. They went out from just after the war until just before he died in 2004. His name's spelt differently to the cricketer, too (I could make a joke here about losing the ashes, but I can't be bothered).

He was 95, so he was too old to be any use as a bone marrow donor anyway, and the lung cancer that killed him had spread to his bones.

The gang who used his body altered the age and cause of death on the death certificate.

I've been told by a pathologist (who didn't know the story, and at first refused to believe I hadn't made it up) that his marrow would give anyone cancer if they didn't have it already.

Shrink-to-fit drainpipe jeans legs

Seven firms across New York, Philadelphia and New Jersey were at it, and they sold bits – bones, skin, arteries, ligaments – from 1,400 bodies to transplant clinics all over the world for four years before they were caught. If it was bones, they used to jam white plastic plumber's pipe between the stubs of bone that were left and stitch everything up afterwards.

Incredibly, this wasn't a one-off – also in 2004, the owner of a cremation company in San Diego was sentenced to 20 years for doing the same thing.

And a mafia funeral director in Elizabeth NJ got caught out using a model of double-decker casket that he'd invented to dispose of victims of mob hits along with the legitimate occupants.

Six feet under/under six feet

Then there's James Hines, the albino soul and R&B guitarist made-to-measure for his coffin, or as CNN put it:

> "a former employee had alleged since his death that he was 'too tall for his coffin and that the funeral home took extreme measures to make him fit'".

When his widow chose the coffin she wondered if it would be big enough (he was six foot seven at that point) and the funeral director said

> "Yes that will be perfect."

When the South Carolina coroner's office exhumed him, they found that his legs had been cut off between ankle and calf, and the severed sections laid in the foot of the coffin (it was an open casket funeral, but only the upper half was open, in that peculiar stable door configuration that they do in America).

The standard American casket's inside measurement is 80 inches, which explains the funeral director thinking it would be "perfect" for Hines's 79 inches, but presumeably the padding took up more space than he expected.

The usual undertaker's bodge for this problem is to raise the knees or bend the legs to one side, remove some of the padding at the foot end, and raise the head and chest up on padding at the other end, but cutting the feet off would certainly be quicker.

Cutting out the middleman

In Poland they have a government grant to cover funeral costs, and with the arrival of the free market in the in the 80s, it became standard practice for undertakers pay off ambulance crews and doctors with vodka to make sure they got the job.

It's called "skinhunting" – skora = fur, skin, pelt – although as used here, perhaps scalp is the closest equivalent. It happened across what used to be Yugoslavia, too.

As competition hotted up, undertakers started to give out free mobile phones to call in the tip, and cash replaced vodka for the bung. Healthcare professionals are badly paid in Poland, and by 2000 they were getting a lot more in 'skin' money than wages.

There was a kind of Wild West goldrush fuelled by the funeral grants, which saw doctors and paramedics switch from pre- to post-mortem service as they capitalised on their 'portable skills' in the new economic climate by going into the undertaking business.

In Lodz, the inevitable tendency of unrestricted competition to result in a monopoly was brought about by the outstandingly efficient business methods of a local Mr Big, who apparently started out by taking over his mother's florist shop, followed, with remarkable rapidity, by most of her competitors, the funeral firms they supplied, the hospital mortuaries, and the presidency of the regional undertaker's association.

The new circumstances fostered a keen spirit of competition amongst ambulance crews and doctors, but it seems an ideological shift in job description took place when one team who were meant to deliver an old woman to a hospital outside the Lodz area couldn't see the point of taking her there when she was going to die anyway, and they'd then miss out on their 'skin' money.

So they drove her straight to the undertakers and waited outside until she pegged out.

The next step in this process of marketplace streamlining and efficiency was for emergency medical staff to stimulate the supply side of the equation by giving anyone plausible a muscle relaxant called Pavulon, normally used to stop the heart and lungs during chest surgery.

Without a heart/lung machine to take over, the patient dies a horrible death, being fully conscious and unable to draw a breath or move a muscle as they die. The soaring Pavulon consumption was covered by forged prescriptions.

The emergency callcentre ambulance dispatchers did their bit to drum up trade too – they'd delay sending off ambulances, to give accident victims a better chance of becoming fatalities (but entering a time more in keeping with their job title in the log).

This all came to light in 2002 because a reporter on a national paper who was researching the stitching up of funeral grants payments between doctors and undertakers heard a rumour about what was happening in Lodz.

When he checked, he found that the previous year's use of Pavulon was more than double that of Warsaw, for a population half the size.

The trial of ambulance drivers that followed was originally going nowhere, because the accused just denied everything, but it was blown wide open by a police sting operation against someone higher up.

A former morgue manager, who had bought the morgue and run it as a business after the fall of communism, was, it seems, unhappy because according to him he had originally been the senior partner in a cosy deal with Mr Big to divvy up funeral custom, and resented Mr Big unilaterally restructuring the cut in his own favour. He had supposedly been threatening to go public about 'skinhunting' and claim it was all organised by Mr Big.

It seems that when the police heard about this, they sent a plainclothes policeman to represent himself as a hitman to the disgruntled (self-styled) former partner, and to offer to solve his problems by 'taking out' Mr Big.

When the disgruntled (self-styled) former partner – let's call him "No.2" (although his name is Jacek Tomazski, and Mr Big is Witold Skrzydlewski) – agreed, and met to hand over the fee, they arrested him and charged him with attempted murder.

This was all revealed in a documentary called "Necrobusiness", which came out in 2008 and has been shown everywhere except Poland. Mr Big apparently agreed to be interviewed on that basis, but of course, they have YouTube in Poland, and Necrobusiness has been available with Polish subtitles ("Lódzi Nekrobiznes") since the minute it came out.

"No.2" went to prison, for endangering human life, as did two doctors from the original case, together with two ambulance drivers, for murder.

Mr Big is still Mr Big, and of course he wasn't charged with anything in the first place, so perhaps it might be that this is a story about antiethical health care, more than underworld undertaking, but it's still certainly very much about the business of death.

The original police estimate was that 50,000 'skins' were hunted over 10 years, with 70 murders committed as part of that, but the prosecution said as many as 20,000 could have been murdered during that period.

Military millinery

If you watch the documentary, one thing you might notice is how tiny the crowns of uniform peaked caps are in Poland. The prison warders, court attendants and police all look like they're wearing novelty hats for some kind of paramilitary kids' party.

It's just the opposite with those sorts of hats in Russia, though, and with service berets in America. In those cases, both the headgear and the badges on them are absurdly large.

Best Seller – Miniature Casket Business Card Holder (Gold) $21.95

Perusing trade journals for scandal and criminality revealed the existence of an unexpected treasure trove of funeral-themed memorabilia on offer to a select client base. (Yes, American trade journals, of course. Civilians here can't get hold of copies of The Funeral Service Journal or The Embalmer at all, and there's bugger-all to look at on the websites unless you're a member.)

Books for specialised tastes ("Carved-Panel Hearses: An Illustrated History 1933-1948"), lapel pins, desk ornaments, key fobs, humorous wall plaques, in fact, everything you might expect to find in the classifieds of any trade magazine.

A previously unconsidered source of light reading to fill odd moments of unfilled leisure time is also catered for – celebrity death certificates. They're all there: "the world's best-known movie stars, writers, directors, singers" and, last but not least, "gossip columnists".

And which best-known names in particular are dangled before you to whet your appetite?

The Marx Brothers, Charles Bronson, and – of course! – Jim Backus.

Who could fail to be gripped by a previously unsuspected urge to know exactly what put The Millionaire from Gilligan's Isle on the slab once they'd seen that name?

(Can't wait to find out, now that your interest's been piqued?

Well, the voice of Mr Magoo was silenced by... pneumonia.)

As for the rest of the merchandise, the lapel pins come in varieties like "The Gold Plated Shovel Tie Clasp and Matching Lapel Pin Set" or ones featuring the ever-popular old-timey Horse-Drawn Funeral Carriage Motif.

And to go with the best-selling Miniature Casket Business Card Holder, there's the matching Personalized Miniature Casket, in exquisitely handcrafted pine, tastefully emblazoned with your company logo or monogram; which also makes the Lapel Pins Casket Combo such a winner for the customer with an eye for a bargain – the full set of lapel pins (including the Embalming Artistry Professional Pin), complete with a miniature casket to keep them in, assuming you can manage to resist wearing them all at once, all the time.

Hearses crop up a lot, and not just on the pins in the Lapel Pin and Casket Combo.

For instance, precision die cast models for desk or collectibles cabinet display are available of everything from the 1934 Buick Miller-Bodied Art Carved Funeral Coach and the 1937 Studebaker (which in the 1:24 option comes accessorised with a to-scale coffin, trestle and wreath holder set), to the Streamlined Classic 1954 Henney-Packard Landaulet.

These would also, clearly, make perfect gifts for the funeral-mad young undertaker of tomorrow to play with (in a suitably staid and dignified way) and cherish.

As for the humorous badges and plaques, try

> "YOUR UNDERTAKER IS THE LAST PERSON TO LET YOU DOWN"

> (with a line drawing of a spade, just in case the joke isn't immediately obvious).

> "AlLL MEN ARE CREMATED EQUAL"

> (which you will notice, I have pinched for use in this book)

"XXXX'S MORTUARY: HOME OF THE EXTREME MAKE OVER"

XII

The History of Undertaking

I was going to begin by saying that important funerals in Britain were traditionally organised by the College of Heralds, which is how books on undertaking often begin their coverage of the history of the trade.

Books on undertaking fall into three categories, the first being books by undertakers, which usually consist of funny and sad 'salt of the earth' stories, plus some potted history, which usually gives the family firm undeserved prominence from a strictly historical point of view.

These typically portray undertakers as a cross between social workers and public benefactors, and the author often uses the opportunity to decry the second category of books about undertaking: books by outsiders that make out undertakers are money-grabbing conmen, heartless jackals who prey on people in their hour of grief.

Then there's academic works; sociological, historical or whatever.

"Big Fry's Come Into Town"

The first two categories often trace the origins of undertaking to the College of Heralds, a medieval organisation concerned with coats of arms and aristocratic families.

It crops up in a Bond book, the film of which starred George Lazenby in a kilt and a frilly cravat, generally considered the worst Bond of all, and chosen because Chubby Broccoli saw him in a choc advert on TV. (*On Her Majesty's Secret Service*, Eon Films, 1969)

The origins of undertaking owe as much to what the heralds didn't do as what they did, however, (as I'll explain later), and they're not actually called the College of Heralds (or the Royal College of Heralds) either.

The College of Arms (and Ian Fleming got it right in the Bond book) was and is the repository of all wisdom on the genealogy of the ruling class of the British Isles since the Middle Ages, and ultimate arbiter on questions of protocol and precedence for toffs.

They've certainly got everything to do with what we now call state funerals, and the rigmarole of the funerals they organised served as a model for the Victorian funeral in its heyday.

The College of Arms is a part of the Royal Household in charge of organising ceremonial events, but they make their money from "granting" coats of arms to people and organisations in the UK and Commonwealth. (For those of you not familiar with the term, the Commonwealth is what they call the British Empire now that there's some choice involved in being in it.)

Circular logic

That involves deciding whether you're a "fit person" to "bear arms", and then "drawing up" a coat of arms for you.

Fit person originally meant a gentleman, which to start with seems to have been supposed to be self-explanatory, but as far as the only recorded definition for the heralds themselves (from the time of James I (or VI of Scotland), it means having an annual income from property or "moveable wealth".

In other words, having enough money to keep up a certain lifestyle, and perhaps not incidentally, pay the heralds' fees.

The heralds also open and close parliament, but the highpoints of their existence are royal funerals and coronations. They're in charge of the organisation, or rather their boss is: the "Earl Marshal", a hereditary job (of course) for the Duke of Norfolk's family since 1135.

(Yes, the same Duke of Norfolk that is Anthony Noel Kelly's uncle – the artist that got the lawbooks rewritten to make stealing body parts a felony.)

Aside from organising the whole thing and being in charge of all the details, the heralds walk in front of everyone else in the funeral procession holding up bits of the monarch's armour and a tabard with the Royal arms embroidered on it.

Which, strangely enough, via the feather plumes on the helmet of the suit of armour, supplied the inspiration for one of the quintessential elements of the Victorian funeral and a multimillion pound global industry associated with it (see Chapter XII, *The History of Undertaking*), and even persists as a faint echo down the ages to today, in the funeral director's walking in front of the hearse with a silver-topped cane.

The heralds organised funerals for the aristocracy as well as royalty, and one of the reasons for the rise of undertakers was the heralds' refusal to do it for anyone else. They then found themselves out of a job with the aristocracy when the undertakers undercut their prices.

Elements of the ceremonial and paraphernalia of the funeral procession and the roll call of strangely-attired and accoutred officials that the heralds' self-fulfilling job creation scheme produced were appropriated by undertakers, and by the 19th century, people were bankrupting themselves to pay for it all.

We might ask, though, where the College of Arms funeral rigmarole came from?

The best-recorded funerals from before they took responsibility are royal funerals, and the aristocratic funerals we have records of were similar.

In medieval times, burial generally followed death as soon as possible, but there were many reasons why royal funerals were delayed. The first royal funeral as Europe emerged from the Dark Ages was a lesson in what could happen if things were left for too long.

William the Conqueror fell ill at Rouen in 1087, apparently after doing himself some kind of a mischief going riding too soon after eating, when the pommel of his saddle injured his overhanging paunch.

When he died shortly afterwards, most of the court cleared off to batten down the hatches until it became obvious who was going to succeed him – but not before pinching everything of value in the palace, including all the furniture and the clothes off the corpse.

His son and heir wasn't there because he was away fighting in the king of France's army – against William – and William's half-bother, 'Bishop Odo', was in prison – where William had put him. Medieval monarchs were traditionally more keen on being feared than respected, but William took it to extremes.

Only a "lowly knight" was left to arrange the funeral, and the body was eventually taken to Caen Abbey (founder: William the Conqueror).

As you may have gathered from the fact that his paunch overflowed his saddle, William was a big man, and when they came to put him in the stone sarcophagus built for him, it turned out to be too small.

When they attempted to stuff him in anyway, it became obvious that part of the reason he was too big was a consequence of the interval between death and the funeral being too long, because the gas-filled abdomen burst, and the subsequent stench cleared the building in an unfunereal rush.

Powerful lesson as this type of thing may have been, there was often a problem in implementing a rapid royal burial – the fact that medieval courts used to spend a lot of time on the road.

That was for two very good reasons. At a time when a monarch's rule depended to a great extent on his martial strength, it was a good idea from the monarch's point of view for the ruling class around the country to be reminded of that martial strength by having him and his court turn up on the doorstep.

Remember that the nobles that the court consisted of were also knights in armour, all accompanied by their supporters; an armoured knight on horseback at that time being the equivalent of a tank regiment in WWII.

Caravan site camping fee

The second reason was monetary. Having what was in effect an army and its camp followers camped in and around your house certainly encouraged respect for the king, but that kind of reminder of royal might was also a powerful disincentive to tax evasion.

More importantly, food, drink, and stabling for the court and its retinue of servants, grooms, squires, pages and horses was a massive expense, and time on the road staying elsewhere was all time someone else was paying for it.

So there were very good reasons why a medieval monarch's body might be a long way from where it needed to be buried, and given the state of the roads, no very rapid way of getting it there, and the same applied to the mourners, who mostly consisted of the court, which was just as far from wherever the burial needed to be because the court travelled with the monarch.

This is why embalming was part of the funeral protocol, but as we've seen, the effectiveness of the techniques used was often less than adequate.

Full Wax Body Double

The problem was that the body needed to be on show when it might not be in any condition to be on show, and the answer was for there to be two bodies: the real one, which could be sealed up inside a casket, and an effigy that could stand in for the real thing at all the rituals bar the actual burial.

I'm proud to say that this was an English invention, and the first time we know that it was used was for the funeral ceremonies of Edward II in 1327.

And, as with the plumes on the helmet carried at the head of the funeral procession and the herald that carried it inspiring elements of undertaking down the ages, a modern version of the funeral effigy is still in popular use.

Edward's father ('the First') actually got the first royal 'open casket job', in which the body was displayed while on tour and at the funeral ceremony, but they didn't do that with his son's body. Maybe EI's embalmers had promised more than they could deliver, and the open casket idea didn't work out too well in practice, but there may have been other reasons.

Edward II had 'favourites' that he unwisely favoured over his wife and the court, and was deposed after his wife left him, and her father (the king of France) sent her back with an army to sort Edward out.

Il H.O.O.Q

None of the English nobles would fight on Edward's behalf and he was forced to abdicate. He died in Gloucestershire. His funeral took place at Gloucester Abbey after lying in state for a month at Berkeley Castle, where it was rumoured he had been murdered (but it seems the famous red-hot poker story is just that, and more to do with contemporary attitudes to bisexuality than historical accuracy).

Fieschi business

An effigy was made and displayed on top of the coffin at Berkeley, in the procession, and at the funeral.

A copy of a letter that was sent to Edward III ten years after his father's death might explain why. It's a genuine document of the period from an Episcopalian archive. It was sent by an Italian priest in Avignon, and it claims that Edward II escaped from Berkeley Castle to Ireland and then travelled to Italy, where he lived in an abbey.

Another theory is that the embalming left the body unrecognisable.

The King is Dead, Long Live the King

Edward II's effigy was dressed in the royal coronation robes as a representation of the god-given royal right to rule, which didn't die with the king, but passed on to his successor.

The tradition of displaying coronation robes as part of funeral ritual had started with Henry II a hundred years earlier, and it also caught on with the other royals in France. All the Norman/Plantagenet kings from William to Edward III ruled northern France as well as England, which was why William's capital was Rouen, not London.

The first one who spoke English was Edward IV... so, better late than never. Even if it did take 400 years.

The use of royal effigies in France was combined with the coronation robes/right to rule idea to produce a bizarre example of collective insanity whereby the effigy was treated as if it actually was: a) the monarch it depicted, and b) alive.

The succession of power happened at the last of a series of court funeral banquets where courses were served to an effigy sat at the head of the table in coronation robes, with the heir apparent on its right. Power passed to the heir when (s)he rose from the table at the end of the final meal.

Head of the Household

The Ancient Greeks and Romans had the custom of having a funeral supper in the family home with an effigy of the deceased at the head of the table. Afterwards the head of the effigy was put on a shelf by the front door in a line-up of other dead relatives.

The earliest royal effigies were made from wood, leather and straw, with a wooden head carved and painted to be as realistic as they could make it, but Henry VI's effigy (1461) had a wax face that was cast from a life or death mask, and that became standard practice.

There's a collection of heads from royal effigies in Westminster Abbey today (but not on a shelf by the front door).

Meanwhile...

The actual royal bodies were embalmed and put in 'cere cloth'; linen dipped in tar, oil and molten wax which was wrapped tightly around the body like swaddling clothes on a baby. The viscera were usually buried where the embalming took place, but sometimes they were put in jars and kept with the body.

The body was then soldered into a lead coffin which fitted the body just as tightly, with the heart often being removed and soldered into its own container, which was sometimes attached on the top of the coffin.

Unusually, Richard II's face was left showing, and he was displayed in his peek-a-boo casket at his funeral (1399).

Early medieval royal bodies, William's included, were sewn into gilded or decorated leather after they were wrapped in cere cloth, as were those of the aristocracy, who kept the tradition up until the end of the Middle Ages.

All the kings of England from Edward II to James I had effigies, and their queens and heirs. The last effigy to be paraded in a funeral procession wasn't royal, though, just the opposite: it was Oliver Cromwell's.

The fashion lasted even longer on the continent – 1786 in Germany, with Frederick the Great.

Just as the Victorian use of plumes and the undertaker preceding the hearse are distant echoes of medieval ceremony, there's a kind of update of the royal effigy that exists in contemporary funeral custom, here and in America.

Before and after

Even with an open casket, the now obligatory photo of the deceased is displayed, usually on a table adjacent to the casket, but sometimes actually on the closed half of the casket lid.

In Britain we tend to go more for a photo display at the wake rather than at the crematorium or church, showing the high points of the life that's just ended.

The Common Funeral and the Common Coffin

So, that's how royal deaths were dealt with before the College of Arms was founded in 1484, but what did everyone else do?

For those who could afford it, the same as they did after 1484 – that is, as much as they could to copy the royals – is the simple answer.

Aristocratic funerals were also organised by the heralds anyway, and funeral fashion, just like other fashions before we had a fashion industry and glossy magazines, was copied from their 'betters' by the rest of society as far as circumstances allowed.

Not too different from now really, except that the 'betters' today aren't 'better' by an accident of birth, but by the accident of fame.

Once again, what's written on this subject often tends to recirculate the same points without much consideration: wearing black for funerals and mourning is an ancient tradition that starts with the Romans, on a superstitious level it's about making yourself invisible to possibly confused and hostile spirits of the dead, and 'Mutes' – professional mourners who walk in the funeral cortège and carry black-wrapped staves – came from the Roman lictors who walked in funeral processions, etc.

Look on the internet, where the same nuggets of information from the literature are endlessly recycled in different combinations.

The trouble with all that is that wearing black at funerals and black being associated with death isn't such an ancient tradition, and neither are Mutes, or "widow's weeds", or wearing black hatbands or veils, or any of the rest of it.

These were actually developments of funeral fashion which mostly coincided with the appearance of the undertaking trade, but that was probably more to do with the undertakers' new class of client and a general change in fashions of the time than undertakers being some kind of gurus of graveside style.

We know from contemporary illustrations that men wore black hoods at funerals from the end of the 1300s until the late 16th century; medieval style cowls with a collar that covered the shoulders and a pony tail tube of cloth coming from the top of the head at the back. They were worn with capes, which continued as funeral fashion until the early Victorian period.

Black wasn't particularly associated with funerals to begin with perhaps, but people would have worn their best clothes, and black was a colour worn by most professions: priests, lawyers, doctors, academics. Not just the colour, but the hood and cape, or gown, are of course also academic and professional ceremonial dress.

Black clothes were also a sign of status because black dye was the most expensive to make.

Women didn't go to funerals until the start of the 20th century, and the mourning colour for women was originally white.

This would only be for important or wealthy people, though. Most people wouldn't have many clothes to choose from, and the funeral would be something done soon as possible, with little ceremony. With the body being kept at home, and ordinary families living very closely together, often in one room, there wouldn't be much choice.

The body would be attended round the clock until burial, partly out of respect for the spirit of the deceased and partly to watch for signs of life – as I've already said, there would be no doctor to certify death, and there was next to no systematic knowledge of physiology or vital signs anyway.

This watching over the body (hence 'wake') wasn't necessarily such a gloomy business. The medieval clergy tried to stamp out the traditional fun and games that went on, but they continued in country districts until the Puritan era:

> "At the funeralls in Yorkeshire, to this day, they continue the custome of watching and sitting-up all night till the body is interred. In the interim some kneel downe and pray (by the corps), some play at cards, some drink & take Tobacco: they have also Mimicall plays and sports e.g. they choose a simple young fellow to be a Judge, then the Suppliants (having first blacked their hands by rubbing it under the bottome of the Pott), beseech his lordship and smutt all his face. They also play likewise at Hott-cockles."
>
> *Remaines of Gentilisme and Judaisme*, John Aubrey, 1686

"Hot cockles" was apparently a violent version of Blind Man's Buff which involved the blindfolded victim being hit while trying to identify the author of each blow. (And according to Nigel Barley in his anthropological compendium of death customs, the Buffs were aimed at the Blind Man's privates.)

After the vigil the body would be taken to the church in the parish coffin. One coffin did for everyone, and was only used to transport the body to the church for the funeral mass, and then to the graveside. The body would then be buried in its shroud.

What happened to the soul, not the body, was what bothered them in those days. A last confession and extreme unction (the last blessing with sacred oil by the priest), followed by a funeral mass with prayers for the soul of the departed were the things that mattered, so the burial was a very perfunctory affair.

After being carried in the communal coffin, the body was buried in an unmarked grave in what was effectively a communal graveyard. From time to time, anonymous bones would be removed to make room for more burials, and these would then be stored in a communal charnel house ('charnel' from Latin via Old French, meaning carcass or body, as is 'carnal').

After the burial there would be a celebration centred around a funeral meal. The medieval funeral meal was, even more than the church high holidays and feast days, one occasion when the rule of grinding poverty was temporarily relaxed, and ordinary people ate and drank well, however briefly.

This was perhaps the origin of the over-the-top Victorian funeral customs which saw poor people bankrupt themselves rather then endure the shame of not putting on a good funeral.

How was it paid for? Just like the coffin and the grave, it was communal. Everyone paid what they could into a fund administered by the parish burial guild, which was then drawn on as needed, regardless of what the individual or his family had paid in.

The most traditional part of the medieval funeral feast would be simnel cake, apparently from the Latin word for 'fine flour', which itself came from the Greek word that gave us 'semolina' in English – another funeral tradition from the Greeks via the Romans. (That's flour which is fine in the sense of 'superior', rather than being finely ground, meaning flour made from wheat.)

Until the Victorian period, barley was the default crop over much of the British Isles because it tolerates poor soil and cold weather better than wheat.

Simnel cake had associations with death and religion because it was eaten at Easter (and so also with the life to come), all very appropriate for a funeral.

Here's a recipe:

Medieval Simnel Cake

You will need: 2 mixing bowls, mixing spoon, measuring cup, scales, baking tray, tablespoon, teaspoon, knife, fork, rolling pin, clingfilm, whisk or eggbeater, pastry brush.

Ingredients:

Pastry

3 cups of plain flour
1 cup of suet or lard (from the fridge)
6 tablespoons of water (from the fridge)

Mix the flour and salt in a bowl. Cut up the suet and add it to the mixture, chopping it together with a knife until the pieces are the size of grains of rice. Add the water a tablespoon at a time, mixing with a fork, until it forms a ball. Wrap the ball in clingfilm (saranwrap) and put it in the fridge for half an hour. While it's cooling make the filling.

Mixture
100g ground almonds
150g currants
150g chopped up stoned prunes
60g candied peel
60g chopped walnuts
1/2 teaspoon cinnamon
1/2 teaspoon ground cloves
1/2 teaspoon nutmeg
1/2 teaspoon white pepper
1/2 teaspoon dried ginger
1 tablespoon honey

Mix the walnuts with the spices in a bowl and add the tablespoon of honey. Mix in the ground almonds and the fruit.

Sprinkle flour on a chopping board or table and rub some on a rolling pin. Roll out the pastry ball until it's about 3/4 inch (2 cm) thick.

Cut pastry into six squares about 3-4 inches (8-10 cm) on each side. Put one square on a greased baking tray and add 4 others to it to make a box, smearing water on the edges beforehand, and then pinching and crimping the edges together. Add the filling and pour 1/2 a tablespoon of warm water into the middle before putting the last square on top, crimping the edges and piercing with a fork. If the filling doesn't come to the top, crimp the edges more until it does.

Put the oven on at 180 C (360 F).

Glaze
> pinch of saffron
> 2 tablespoons boiling water
> 4 tablespoons honey
> 1 egg white

Dissolve the saffron in the boiling water, mix in the honey and then beat in the egg white. Paint the pie with the glaze, then put it in the middle of the pre-heated oven and bake for about 30 mins. until the pastry is hard. Remove, and when cool, slide a knife or metal spatula under the pie and transfer to a serving plate. Slice and eat when cold.

This would have been a very superior simnel cake in the Middle Ages, affordable only by royalty and the richest and most powerful aristocrats and clergy.

Spices and almonds were fabulously expensive because they had to come all the way from the Holy Land or the Spice Islands (the Mollucas/Malaku, in Indonesia) via Venice, and their availability depended on wind and weather, the time of the year, who was at war with who at any point on the way, whether a crusade was in progress, and the avoidance of pirates or unfriendly naval forces.

If you want to make a simnel cake that only royalty would have eaten, add dried figs and use sugar instead of honey – sugar on the table was a real sign of opulence and privilege in Britain until Georgian times.

And yes, as you'll have gathered from the amounts of honey, they had very sweet tooths in the Middle Ages, as they did all the way up until the First World War. Even bread used to have malt syrup added until it would have been unpleasantly sweet to a modern palate.

> "The only thing that ever really frightened me during the war was the U-boat peril." Winston Churchill

The WWI submarine blockade had an unexpected and long-lasting effect on British tastes. Not only was sugar rationed, the very idea of dietary indulgence was considered unpatriotic, and recipes were adjusted accordingly – all reinforced by the reprise of that situation in WWII. In neutral Scandinavia, bread, and many processed foods (blood pudding, for instance) remain unpleasantly sweet for a Brit to this day, as (excepting bread), in the US, unaffected by rationing, and historic land of plenty.

There was another culinary association with funerals and mourning that was shared by aristocracy and commoners, and which lasted from medieval times until after the Restoration: rosemary.

Mourners would wear sprigs of it in their hats, and carry it in the funeral procession to throw into the grave after the burial service. This might have had something to do with rosemary's use in drying and pickling meat, and so as a religious symbol of the incorruptibility of the soul, or on a more practical level, its scent might have masked one sign of the corruption of the actual body at the funeral.

Back to Black

It's difficult to establish with certainty exactly when black came to be the definitive colour of mourning and funerals in Britain (or strictly speaking, perhaps that should be 'lack of colour'), but it was definitely popularised by undertakers.

Royal funerals had their own rules and traditions, but those traditions were sometimes very colourful.

For instance, for Henry VIII's pall (the cloth draped over his coffin) they used sky blue and cloth of gold, and for Elizabeth I, purple. Previously the equally colourful royal coat of arms was used.

Illustrations of Tudor and Elizabethan funerals show black garments worn by male mourners, particularly hoods and cloaks for the attendants of the hearse, and the use of black ribands and drapery, but the first use of black for a royal pall was that of Charles II, a hundred years later.

It seems Queen Anne of France was the first woman to wear mourning costume of black rather than white, in 1498, also unusual in that the entire outfit was of one colour. Widows traditionally wore a white headdress and chinpiece together with white cuffs, apparently inspired by those worn by nuns, as a symbol of their newly imposed condition of chastity.

What we do know is that black definitely did come into its own as the colour for funerals and mourning – clothing, hearse cloths, draping the home and church – in the early 1600s.

This coincided with two developments in the business of death: the staging of aristocratic-style funerals by commoners of the new merchant class, who weren't allowed to use the heralds, and the appearance of undertakers.

It was also around this time that the heralds themselves began to employ undertakers, presumably because the dissolution of the monasteries and the Reformation meant that the monks who had traditionally been responsible for dealing with royal or aristocratic bodies were persona non grata or even persona non-existent.

By 1689, the heralds were being paid to provide their services by an undertaker, rather than the other way round. That was William Russell, often called the first undertaker. (But the Bodleian library in Oxford has an undertaker's trade card of 1675 or so, for a William Boyce "at the sign of the White Hart and Coffin in the Great Old Bayley".)

The medieval religious idea of the body not being important, and the anonymous communal approach to burial, with payment for the burial out of the communal parish guild, had been replaced by the idea of ordinary people being treated as individuals, not just royalty and aristocrats.

This originated from the mid 14th century, and the cause was the Black Death – so many died, and labour became so scarce, that it became essential for people to be able to move around, or no crops would be planted or harvested, and everyone, including the ruling class, would starve.

People could leave their villages to work where they could get the best wage, and were no longer tied in bondage to the lord of their manor.

The Black Death hit Britain worst, which is why feudal rule was weakened in Britain; whereas treating people like peasants – literally, as someone's personal property because they were born on his land – continued on the Continent.

The first undertakers were joiners, workers in wood who were tradesmen, lower in the working class hierarchy than craftsmen like carpenters and cabinet makers, and they were the men who would have made the communal coffins for the use of the parish.

They were contracted to make individual coffins for those who now saw themselves as individuals and had the money to mark themselves out in this way.

Henry's dissolution of the monasteries and creation of new nobles (often given, in a neat circularity, the church land) who were not part of the self-enclosed network of aristocratic descent finally broke the continuity of the system whose hold had begun to be loosened by the Black Death. The pre-existing aristocratic hierarchy and all its gradations and orders of precedence was of course policed by the heralds.

Another thing that appeared in the 1600s was a fashion for night-time funerals, and funeral processions with flaming torches and churches filled with hundreds of candles. The traditional explanations for wearing black might start to make sense here – wearing black at night, and in a church or home draped with black would certainly be good camouflage against attracting the attention of malevolent ghosts. But then again, if there actually was some idea of that, why would you then draw attention to yourself by carrying a flaming beacon on the way to the church and the grave?

Previously, night-time funerals had been a special privilege reserved for people of rank and distinction, but now anyone who could pay for it could have one. Another reason for their popularity, and maybe the main one, was that the heralds wouldn't have anything to do with them, so this would be a way for cash-strapped aristos to avoid the massive fees the heralds charged. The aristocracy then set the fashion for everyone else.

Since the heralds would not organise these funerals, or any funerals for commoners, the role of the joiners who supplied the coffins expanded to fill the need.

Black really was "the new black"

The burgeoning use of black at funerals and for mourning also coincided with a more general fashion for black that gripped British society, a fashion that first appeared in the Spanish court and then spread to Holland. Think of the paintings of the time, with moody-looking men with pointy beards showing their expensive lace linen to best effect against black clothes, and similarly of the women, who were also keen to show off their fashionably pale complexions.

The new trade of undertaking served a new clientèle, a class of society that had only recently come into being: the merchant class, or what would become the middle class, made newly wealthy by the explosion in trade from the New World and England's naval dominance of the trade routes.

This was the first time that there were people who were rich and powerful who weren't part of the aristocracy or clergy, and they were just as keen to show off their wealth and power in life – mansions like palaces, the most expensive and fashionable clothes and possessions, portraits painted by the best and most fashionable artists – as in death.

It would hardly be surprising that if there was a fashion for black in life, there should also be one in death, particularly if there was also a new trade around to capitalise on that fashion.

Human funeral bling

Also around the 1600s, mourning cloaks replaced hoods for funeral wear, and a tradition began for these to be supplied as gifts by the bereaved family; as gloves (originally in white) and mourning rings (as memento mori) already were.

Poor parishioners were invited to bulk out the funeral procession and fill the church, and they all got cloaks and gloves too, as well as a feed at the wake.

They would originally have been tenants from the family estate, and, like candles on a birthday cake, the number present originally commemorated the age of the dearly departed; but crowding the local plebs in, with the cost of their attendant perks, ended up as a kind of display of money-to-burn ostentation.

The cloaks and gloves would go straight back to the undertaker, acting as a kind of post-mortem pawnbroker. Undertakers also did house clearances, discounting whatever they estimated the value as from the cost of the funeral.

Joiners had found themselves doing a job that had developed as their job description had expanded, until the undertaking of funeral organisation eclipsed the joinery.

The use of professional mourners, or Mutes, supplied, of course, by the undertaker, also appeared at this time, together with the custom for a pair of them to stand either side of the threshold to the home before the funeral.

In the early 1700s black cloth drapery began to be used in quantity to drape the home, the funeral bier or hearse, and the church. It was of a special kind, not just black in colour, but of a particularly appropriate finish – a specially-woven silk with a crinkled texture that filled out draperies and made them hang well, and with a suitably funereal lack of shine or showiness. The special fabric with the very special qualities was called crape.

First just the coffin, then cloaks, the hearse, Mutes, black drapery: all supplied by the joiner turned undertaker.

After night-time funerals were prohibited by Charles I because of the "riotous behaviour under cover of darkness" that they encouraged, the carrying of symbolic torches eventually went out of fashion, and the Mutes began to carry symbolic candelabra wrapped in crape, known as Branches.

This continued until the 1780s. After this, the Mutes carried Staves or Wands, poles about four feet in length wrapped in crape and carried vertically, like the staves carried by senators' lictors at Roman funerals.

It was also around the 1780s that undertakers replaced the heralds in organising upper-class funerals, rather then being hired by them. After this, the College of Arms was only involved in the ceremonial surrounding the funeral, rather than the actual details of the 'disposal of the remains' and the funeral itself. This is why they're not, in the fullest sense, predecessors to undertakers in Britain and the US today.

Not only do undertakers here 'undertake' to handle all the details of the funeral and negotiate with the different agencies involved, they also handle the body itself, moving it, storing it on their premises, preparing it, dressing it, and, usually, embalming it.

Undertakers elsewhere organise the funeral and deliver the body on the day, but the storage of the body and embalming is by the local hospital or mortuary.

The Invention of Tradition

From the 1650s onwards there had been a growing general interest in the classical world, in literature, architecture, art, fashion – hence the idea of the Grand Tour, when wealthy young men visited Italy to complete their education in the finer things in life, and to acquire good taste.

This, I think, is where the finding of connections between Roman custom – dark colours for mourning, nighttime funerals with torchlight processions, professional mourners and men carrying staves – and British custom comes from, rather than these things being time-honoured traditions carried on in some way from the Roman occupation of Britain. Vikings and

Anglo-Saxons wouldn't have known what the Romans did, or cared.

The popularity of the Grand Tour and keenness for Ancient Roman and Greek styles reached its height with the Georgians. Georgian Classicism in art, architecture, fashion and literature was restrained and austere, and this was reflected in mourning and funeral fashion.

Georgian funerals and mourning were relatively perfunctory in terms of the time, paraphernalia and, most importantly for undertakers, money involved.
But fashion moves in cycles, and as is the way of these things, as people get bored with one thing and turn to another, what they turn to next tends towards a diametrically opposite pole of fashion in relation to the old style.

The first signs of stirrings against the rule of Classicism appeared in the Regency interest in the bizarre, the exotic and the excessive – in fashion think of Beau Brummell, in architecture, the Brighton Pavilion.

The influence of the Romantic movement in literature led a general fascination with the melancholy and soulful, and this combined with the anticlassical tendency to produce Victorian Gothic.

In parallel with this, funerals and mourning began to be celebrated more thoroughly. And there was a lot more death around to celebrate, too.

Industrialised agriculture – Jethro Tull, Turnip Townsend, Compton's Mule, Reaper McCormick – meant that a larger population could be fed.

The mechanisation of agriculture meant less people were needed to work the land, and people moved to cities to work in the industrialised production of things the increased population wanted (helped on their way by those early versions of 'nudge' social policies, the Enclosure Acts and the Clearances).

The increased population supported by industrialised agriculture had more children, and being crowded together in cities and towns with poor sanitation and rudimentary medical provision meant more death from illness, and, there being almost no health and safety legislation for the factories they worked in, there were also more deaths from accidents there.

As the industrial revolution industrialised the scale of work-related accidents, it also created more possibilities for accidents in day-to-day life, at the same time industrialising the scale of those accidents – the coming of the railways meant railway crashes, rather than horse-drawn coaches losing a wheel for instance.

Iron hulls and steam power meant bigger ships with correspondingly greater loss of life when they sank. Boilers blew up, factory and foundry fires spread to burn down swathes of overcrowded housing, sparks from ships' steam engines set fire to the rigging which still existed on early steam vessels, the flames spread to the dockside warehouses, and huge fires regularly engulfed whole areas of port cities.

Red Sky at Night, Newspaper Proprietor's Delight

Alongside religion, music halls, and gin palaces, one of the favourite communal diversions of the Victorian public was going to watch fires, which took hours or days to burn out and were reported as ongoing entertainment in the daily press.

This was when undertakers really came into their own. The increased interest in death combined with the increased incidence of death led to greater attention to the marking of death. Funerals became more and more elaborate and expensive, with an ever-increasing staff of attendants and more and more paraphernalia and rigmarole, all of which had to be hired from or organised by the undertaker.

A gradually increasing cast of arcane characters purloined from aristocratic funeral ceremony somehow became essential to a respectable send-off, both to attend the bereaved household and to walk in the funeral procession, together with a hearse, its driver and horses, and outriders in frock coats and black jockey's caps on more horses draped in black and wearing ostrich plume head dresses.

The home was swathed in black inside and out, including the doorknocker and knob, with Mutes with Wands on the doorstep either side of the front door. Mutes were undertakers' men wearing frock coats and top hats with 'weepers' – a length of crape tied around and over the hat and hanging down at the back. They also wore three yards-long crape shoulder sashes, like dreary versions of the plaid worn over the shoulder of a regimental Scots piper. A Wand was a six foot pole decorated with an immense crape bow which was held like a stave.

Attendants in the funeral procession also included Mutes with Wands, and others carrying Batons, a kind of field marshal's baton covered in crape, and Truncheons, similar to batons, but larger and held vertically. All the

Mutes could be mounted, on more horses with plume head dresses.

There were also Feather Pages, who carried 'Lids of Feathers' – wire trays measuring three feet on each side covered with ostrich plumes standing vertically.

The hearse itself had a parapet of ostrich plumes, the horses wore plume head dresses and their harness was covered with plumes. Plumes were used in such profligate amounts at funerals that a global industry grew up to supply the demand.

(And all from the plume on a helmet carried by a herald at the head of the medieval funeral procession, multiplied beyond all reason some four hundred years later.)

The coffin was covered by a black baize pall, and the hearse and driver's seats draped in worsted or woollen 'hammer cloth'.

All of which was, of course, charged for accordingly by the undertaker.

In the 1850s the business of draping funeral spaces and buildings in black also expanded, in terms of both quantity and duration – the church used for Lord Eldon's funeral in 1853 was draped for an entire year, a record which was then rapidly beaten by Lord Shaftesbury's, coming in at 14 months.

For the funerals of important public figures or large-scale industrial accidents or other mass tragedies, lampposts and buildings along the route were draped in black, and the cobbles covered in straw to muffle the rattle of metal horseshoes. Shops closed, and church bells tolled a single note (the funeral tocsin) to mark each minute as the procession passed by.

The social pressures for elaborate funerals were so powerful that poor families were often left destitute by the expense involved.

Questions were asked in Parliament:

Chadwick:

> "Are you aware that the array of funerals, commonly made by undertakers, is strictly the heraldic array of a baronial funeral, the two men who stand by the doors being supposed to be the two porters of the castle, with their staves, in black; the man who heads the procession, wearing a scarf, being a representative of a herald-at-arms; the man who carries a plume of feathers on his head being an esquire, who bears the shield and casque (helmet), with its plume of feathers; the pall-bearers, with batons, being representatives of knights-companions-at-arms; the men walking with wands being supposed to represent gentlemen-ushers, with their wands; are you aware that this is said to be the origin and type of the common array usually provided by those who undertake to perform funerals?"

Undertaker:

> "No, I am not aware of it."

Chadwick:

"It may be presumed that those who order funerals are equally unaware of the incongruity for which such expense is incurred?"

Undertaker:

"Undoubtedly they are."

> E. Chadwick (1843) A Supplementary Report on the Results of a Special Enquiry into the Practice of Interment in Towns London: House of Lords, p.51

That the working classes were unable to afford all this was taken as a sign of lack sensitivity or proper respect for the dead, and fear of being associated with such lower class brutishness put even more pressure on people to spend more than they could afford.

Burial clubs, saving societies to put aside weekly money against the eventual cost, were one solution for those who had anything to put by, and the other lifeline for the working poor was guild funerals, for the families of time-served skilled tradesmen who had been apprenticed and joined the guild for their trade.

In these cases, the guild would organise the funeral and, in an echo of medieval parish funerals, the common guild funeral pall would be used, and mourning clothes could be hired from the guild. This was paid for from subscription, and all members were expected to attend guild funerals, or pay a fine.

Skilled tradesmen were the aristocracy of the working class, though, and master craftsmen like cabinet makers earned more than middle class clerks. For the rest of the Victorian working class, a funeral meant keeping the body at home until the first Sunday when a time was available at the parish church, because that was the only day everyone was off work.

That might take two weeks, depending on the local death rate; two weeks sharing a living room, or even the family's single room with the body. The body would be taken on a hand-drawn parish hearse, or bier, which looked like a market trader's barrow, or carried all the way. The family would then put on whatever spread they could afford for the funeral feast; ham and ale being traditional.

For the destitute or unemployed, there was the shame of a pauper's funeral and burial in an unmarked grave.

Obsequey Overdrive

A massively popular young queen's frenzy of grief and mourning on the death of her husband in 1861 added the impetus of royal example. Albert wasn't very popular, but Victoria was.

This, you must remember, was a pre- sucking-on-a-lemon-faced "We are not amused" version of Victoria, when she was a glamorous young cross between Lady Di, the Queen and the Queen Mum all rolled into one. (I mean the post-canonization Lady Di, for those of you old enough to remember the less than pristine reputation Lady Di enjoyed before entering the Place de l'Alma underpass).

These circumstances, together with a pre-existing more strait-laced attitude to conformity and appearance (also inspired by royal example), led to a national obsession with death, funerals and the observance of mourning etiquette. Every detail of a widow's interaction with society and her own family was laid down, and endless elaborations and variations of colour, combination and style of clothing were prescribed.

Full mourning for women (and not just widows) involved swaddling in unrelieved black crape for a year and a day, then bombazine or silk for a year after that. Crape was a heavy silk fabric with a wrinkled appearance that was inflexible and hot to wear, and the sweat it produced leached into the fabric and stained the skin black.

What made it so indispensable for deep mourning was its dead black non-reflective finish. Bombazine was a lighter silk/wool mixture with the wool on the outside to give a dull finish. Even so, the widow was only crape-free for the last three months – the bombazine had to be trimmed with crape for the preceding nine months. Even underwear went into mourning, with black borders and black ribbons. Heavy veils and gloves had to be worn at all times outside the home.

The home itself would also be swathed in black, clocks stopped at the time of death, mirrors turned to the wall, and curtains drawn.

Older widows often continued in full mourning for the rest of their lives, as Victoria did, but protocol otherwise allowed a gradual relaxation after two years, with grey or purple being worn: at first only as edging, then as grey or purple garments with black borders, and eventually as garments of solid grey or purple.

Even babies and toddlers had to be kitted out in black-bordered mourning frocks and bibs, and their crib sheets.

For children's funerals, though, everything had to be white – the coffin, the flowers, the drapery, the ostrich plumes on the horses and the hearse, and the mourners' and undertaker's men's shoulder sashes and weepers. As it also was for the outfit of the tiny corpse, as we see in the very popular photographs of dead children and babies of the time.

Women's mourning dress was unaffected by this white-for-children rule, because women generally didn't attend funerals. This was partly because they were thought to be too upsetting, but also because of the amount of drinking done, in particular by the undertakers' men. Apparently the Doorstep Mutes were the worst offenders, but this might have been due to the fact that yet another ritual of excess associated with funerals, to skimp on which would lose face, was the copious consumption of whisky, and the Doorstep Mutes were first in the line of fire as guests arrived.

Gruesome trousseau

There was also the bizarre custom of Death Weddings – if a bride-to-be died before the wedding, she was buried in her wedding dress, attended by her bridesmaids and maid of honour, and the parson read the wedding service before the burial service.

Women's Work

The actual funeral might have been men's business, considered too upsetting for the delicate swoon-prone female constitution of the time, but every other aspect of mourning ceremony was controlled by the women of the family, including, of course, shopping.

And there was plenty of shopping to be done: for mourning dress, memento mori, mourning jewellery, mourning and funeral cards and stationery, black sealing wax, drapery – there were even mourning ear trumpets, so the hard of hearing could receive condolences via an appropriately funereal accessory.

The One-stop Woe Shop

Among the department stores that began to appear around Britain in the late 1830s was Jay's, whose first branch opened on Oxford Circus (then Regent's Circus) in 1841. Jay's, and their imitators, were a specialist combination of the department store – a British invention, with different domestic goods on different floors all under the same roof – and a French retail innovation, the Maison de Deuil, or House of Mourning.

"Jay's House of General Mourning" sold everything connected with mourning, and also acted as a middleman for the undertakers by offering to organise funerals; in reality simply passing the trade on and charging a premium for doing so.

While undertakers made more and more money from more and more elaborate funerals – by 1870 the total cost of a middle-class funeral could be £1,000, a staggering sum considering that at the time the annual salary of a senior clerk in a City firm was £150, or for a chairman of the board £1,000 – other industries connected with the trade made even more money.

The sun never sets on the British funeral furnishing empire

Massive industries appeared to service the ritual and protocol of mourning, British industries whose products achieved world domination.

The C-word
Jet is a 'gemstone' made from compressed wood from millions of years ago. That sounds like coal though, doesn't it? Yes it does, because that's what jet is, in all but name. 'Gemstone' just means it's used for jewellery.

Unlike diamonds or opals, though, it has much the same appearance before and after it's been turned into jewellery, and its value lies in the fact that it's a kind of goldilocks coal – literally "jet black", so, perfect for mourning jewellery, and soft enough to carve, and taking a good polish, but not as brittle other types of hard coal, so that it's possible to carve detail without flaking.

The best jet comes from Whitby in Yorkshire, and it's the remains of Jurassic era Auracaria trees that were laid down in a salt water swamp and then compressed under layers of shale for millions of years. (The "Monkey Puzzle Tree" from South America, a Victorian garden fashion, is a modern day survivor of the genus). The brown jet found elsewhere is from trees laid down in fresh water.

Jet jewellery began to become popular for mourning at the start of the 19th century, but as so often with funerals and death customs, the Romans were there first.

Jet apparently had supernatural properties for them, being considered effective in warding off the 'evil eye'.

Jet is found in the sea cliffs at Whitby, and the Romans collected it from the beaches there, then took it to York to be worked.

Georgian workshops were in Whitby itself, and as demand for mourning accessories increased in Victorian times, the raw material began to be mined.

There was already a respectable jewellery industry in Whitby exporting across the world, but Victoria's wearing Whitby jet after Albert died sent the business into overdrive. Shortly afterwards, the seams of jet in the mines of Whitby and the North Yorks hills were exhausted, and Spanish jet had to be imported.

The Romans didn't come all the way to Whitby for nothing, though: Spanish jet, like Whitby's other competitors, has a brownish tinge, and can't be worked as finely.

Whitby jet being an essential mourning accessory and the social pressures of being seen to mourn respectably being what they were meant that demand had to be satisfied somehow, and Victorian industry came up with superficially indistinguishable substitutes that that could be quickly and cheaply mass-produced.

Black glass looks the part, but it's slightly too glossy, and hence not funereal enough. Moulded vulcanised (heat-treated) rubber was a much more serious contender, it being possible to achieve the same semi-matt finish and feel, and it also feels warm to the touch like jet.

Luckily for collectors today though, there is a fool-proof test to identify the real thing. As we should all know from watching antiques programmes on TV, if you rub the piece on unglazed porcelain, genuine jet leaves a brown streak.

The industry in Whitby started to falter when they were forced to use Spanish jet, and nose-dived even more under competition from the artificial substitutes. Jet today is once again collected as the action of the waves reveals it from the cliffs at Whitby, as it was in Roman times.

Appropriately enough, what Whitby's famous for today is Goths, particularly the kind that like to drag themselves up in Victorian undertaker gear, crossing into Steam Punk, which is itself a cross between contemporary high tech and Victorian aesthetics (things like ornate cogwheel-ornamented casings for smartphones) and usually involves wearing, for some reason, goggles, often on top hats.

The original attraction is thought to be the fact that Bram Stoker has Whitby as Dracula's arrival point from Transylvania.

The Karoo Sock Puppet

Another funeral fashion commodity that Britain supplied the world with was ostrich feathers. And, as in the case of jet, Britain enjoyed a near-monopoly of the supply and trading of this natural product for the most lucrative period of the craze.

'Plumes', as those in the trade called them, were used in huge amounts for funerals – on the hearse, on the horses, and carried in the procession by the Feather Pages – and a large part of their other main use, the decoration of women's hats, was for mourning millinery.

Plumes were used by the aristocracy and the professions on hats and helmets from the middle ages onwards, and afterwards for (mostly) men's fashion, with a temporary lull when Cavaliers were out of fashion. They became increasingly popular accessories for women's wear from the late Georgian period onwards.

They were always fabulously expensive, being collected from wild birds by African bushmen, and were described in the 1860s as "having a value like that of diamonds", following the boom in demand for funerals, hats and boas.

London had always been the world trade centre for feathers, and in response to the boom in demand, the ostrich was first domesticated in British South Africa.

Curiously enough, the London feather market and the production in South Africa were both controlled by Jewish 'feather millionaires'. In 1890s South Africa, the wealth of famous East End boys made good like the diamond 'Randlords' Barney Barnato and the Joel dynasty was equalled by that of Lithuanian feather millionaires like Max Rose.

Why Lithuanian, you might ask? British Jews would be there because it was a British colony, but what were Lithuanian Jews doing there? And why Lithuanian rather than Polish or Ukranian? Presumably there were refugees from the pogroms going on across the whole Russian empire of the time?

No-one knows. Although Lithuania had a proportionately larger Jewish population than other parts of the Russian empire because it was historically more tolerant, the pogroms following the assassination of

Alexander II in 1881 affected them just as badly, and they joined the Jewish diaspora across the world.

But for whatever reason, most of the Jewish immigrants who arrived in Cape Town were Lithuanian, and to this day, 80% of the Jewish community in South Africa is of Lithuanian origin – I give you the trivia quiz fact that the quintessentially British actors Sid James and Laurence Harvey were both South African litvaks.

The first ostrich farm started off with 80 birds in 1865, exporting 17,000lbs of feathers worth £65,000 (a top middle class professional salary in Britain at the time was £250). By 1913, 700,000 birds were producing a million pounds weight of feathers worth two and three quarter million pounds sterling. And that figure is all the more staggering because by then the British monopoly on ostrich feather production had been broken by farms in the US.

But of course all booms have a bust, and when the end came, it came quickly. 1913 saw a fall in demand for plumes, as the ideal in women's fashion began to move away from the top-heavy look topped off with an extravagant hat, partly because of the influence of new fads in the world of fashion – motor racing and flying.

The First World War finally did for plumes in women's fashion, with Edwardian gaiety suddenly looking out of place, and the military look influencing women's fashion.

Changes making themselves felt in the world of undertaking also had a disastrous effect on the feather trade around the same time.

While feathers are, famously, featherlight, when they get wet it's a different matter. The amounts piled on funeral horses were huge, and while horses' backs and shoulders can take heavy loads, their necks can't, and the headdress harnesses alone weighed eight pounds, and more than double that when wet.

The British Undertakers' Association finally gave in to pressure from the RSPCA and other animal welfare groups by banning the dressing of horses with ostrich plumes in 1916. That counted as a meaningless gesture, though, because by then their horses had been requisitioned by the army anyway.

Undertakers' horses weren't the only ones to suffer. The East End sweat shops of London's feather trade were notorious for the exploitation of children as young as eight, mostly employed glueing 'good' halves from substandard plumes together to produce imitation 'double plumes'.

All that's left today is a building just up the road from a pub mentioned in a nursery rhyme. Plumage House is on Shepherdess Walk in Islington, five minutes from The Eagle pub, which is not actually on the City Road, as you might think from the lyrics of 'Pop Goes the Weasel'. The original Eagle was, but it was demolished at the end of the 19th century. The standard explanation for the rest of the lyrics is confusing, too.

It goes like this: hatters used to pawn, or "pop" the irons, or "weasels", that were used to smooth the plush that hats were made from, to buy food after they'd spent their wages on drink "up and down the City Road, in and out of the Eagle".

That doesn't make sense. If they'd pawned the tools of their trade, they had no means to earn the money to redeem the pledge and get their tools back?

Pop Goes the Weasel goes Pop

Anthony Newley (Mr Elizabeth Taylor at one time, and vocal muse for David Bowie) has an interesting variation. The "official explanation" on his 1961 hit parade version of the rhyme (no.6 in the UK, 85 in the US) has it that hatters popped their weasels to buy liquor on Saturday night.

But Saturday night, I can reveal, was actually when they got paid, so that's when they would have needed to use their wages to pay the pawnbrokers to get their weasels back. Just to make matters worse, like many workers at the time, they were often paid in the pub.

This version would have them redeeming their weasels with their wages, then pawning their weasels to keep drinking, all in the same night. So how could they earn their wages the next week without the tools of their trade?

The rhyme could still make sense, though. I don't know if a hatter's iron was called a weasel, but I do know that an overcoat is called a weasel in rhyming slang.

For American readers, rhyming slang, often known as 'Cockney Rhyming Slang' (although it's used all over the country) was originally a thieves' argot where, typically, a pair of words is used to substitute for another word which rhymes with the second word of the pair. It's a way of communicating which denies the information you're communicating to those outside your community. To that end, often only the first of the pair of words is then used.

So, 'Mutt & Jeff', which rhymes with 'deaf', as in: "He's a bit Mutt & Jeff." becomes "He's a bit Mutton."

In this case, it's 'weasel' from 'weasel & stoat', which rhymes with 'coat'.

Pawning your overcoat when you ran out of money to live on and then redeeming the pledge on payday was a working class financial strategy into the 1960s in Britain. You didn't need your overcoat in the summer, and in the winter you could put your collar up and shiver if it meant putting food on the table.

What remains of the feather trade at the other end of the supply chain is not just bricks and mortar, although there is a lot of that.

The Feather Palaces of Oudtshoorn still adorn what was known as the ostrich capital of the world. They are the mansions that the South African feather millionaires built for themselves, collisions of architectural styles like Scottish baronial and faux chateaux with verandahs, but mostly abandoned now.

Oudtshoorn is still the capital of the ostrich trade, and the trade is looking a lot less shabby than the feather palaces. From a low point of 2,000 birds in 1940, numbers are up to 200,000 today. The business is more to do with low cholesterol meat nowadays, but feathers are still in demand: for feather dusters, used in museums and car factories.

It seems nothing beats ostrich plumes for leaving a dust-free finish, and despite the paint shops of car manufacturers like BMW looking more like NASA satellite assembly areas, the car shells still need a last minute ostrich feather fan dance performed by robots before the paint goes on.

Crêpe de no-shine

Britain's other international success in the industrialisation of mourning was what was known as the 'Black Branch' of the textiles trade.

Crêpe de chine was a type of silk fabric woven to give a puckered appearance, originally imported from France, but the heavy, crumpled, impenetrably dull matt crape deemed so essential everywhere for mourning in the 18th and 19th centuries was a British invention (known in France as crêpe anglais), and from 1820 Courtaulds had a monopoly.

The Courtaulds themselves were also a French import, being Huguenots who arrived in Britain the 1680s. Their mills in Essex supplied the world, and it wasn't until crape went out of fashion that they diversified. This was another case of demand being created and satisfied by the industrial revolution – British crape was better and cheaper than anyone else could make it because of the unique design of the looms invented here, and the fact that they were steam-powered.

Women glow and *perspire*

The massive demand for crape might have had something to do with the fact that at the same time as it being very hot to wear, it shrank to half its original size when it got damp, as it tended to from the perspiration that wearing it produced.

Then there were the servants to be dressed – even the lower middle classes had at the very least one servant.

Then there were also the traditional gifts for all the mourners to be bought: scarves and capes or, later, sashes.

There was also a superstition that it was unlucky to keep mourning clothes, entailing a new set of everything for everyone, every time someone in the family died.

Unlucky for the bereaved: lucky for the textile trade's Black Branch and the Houses of Mourning.

Crape started to go out of fashion from the end of the 1880s, and Courtaulds began experimenting with artificial fibres, inventing Rayon in 1905. As a kind of backwards glance, one of the early developments of Rayon fibre was a lightweight, non-shrink, colourfast crape. They set up the American Viscose Corporation in 1909, and by 1913 they were the biggest producer of manmade fibres in the world.

Mourning crape manufacture finally stopped in 1940, with the closing of the last market for it, France, when the German army occupied Paris.

As far as I can tell, no-one's made crape since 1940, but the name lives on. In India, for some reason, they call chiffon and crepe de chine 'crape', and advertise saris and blouses made from it.

Pomp and Circumstance Marches Off

In terms of elaboration, social obligation and cost, the British funeral (and the British observation of mourning ritual) reached its peak in the 1890s. The decline that followed, gradual to begin with, was at first due to changing social attitudes and developments in the world of women's fashion, but the pace of change forced by the First World War was rapid, permanent, and from the undertaker's point of view, catastrophic.

Undertakers' men of military age volunteered and left for France, and as the war went on, those that were left were conscripted. The army took all the horses, which saw the elaborate plume-trimmed hearse replaced by the new-fangled motor hearse with an unseemly haste normally unheard of in the world of undertaking.

That meant the lucrative sliding scale of charges for horses for the hearse or outriders, based on numbers and elaboration in drapery and plumage disappeared. The reduction in staff meant the undertaker had difficulty supplying the outriders themselves anyway, along with the Feather Pages, Mutes, Wands and all the rest of the bizarre cast of extras he had previously supplied.

And unfortunately for British undertakers, the Great War's bonanza of death didn't translate to a bonanza of trade for undertakers, as the first industrialised modern war, between the states in America, had.

Although industrialised methods of killing – faster-firing and more reliable guns and more productive manufacture of arms and ammunition –produced an exponential increase in battlefield casualties compared to the American Civil War, the larger armies and limited room for manoeuvre in the cramped landscapes of Northern

France and Belgium meant that another invention used in the Civil War also played its part in creating the military mincing machine of trench warfare: barbed wire.

The sheer numbers involved, and the fact that the static nature of trench warfare usually made the collection of bodies impossible meant that the only funerals in Britain were for those of the wounded who lived long enough to be shipped back before they died there.

The nature of this industrial mass-manufacture of death in any case meant that there was often no body to collect, and such remains as there were often got interred by the same shell blast that created them.

There was also a feeling that it was somehow unpatriotic, and in a way disrespectful, to make a fuss about someone dying in their bed at home (as most people still did then) while the flower of the nation's manhood were dying in such spectacularly horrific ways and numbers on the field of battle.

The difficulty of accepting the death of so many young men gone before their time saw a rise in Spiritualism, which also discouraged elaborate funeral displays – you're hardly likely to give someone a big final send-off if you think you're still talking to them whenever you go to the tabernacle or join hands round a table.

As more women worked making shells and explosives, and as they began to replace men in offices, or selling tickets on buses, or doing just about everything but going down coalmines, the last vestiges of Victorian mourning protocol all but disappeared.

The introduction of clothes rationing, a result of the submarine blockade and the priority given to the demands of the armed forces, meant that observing mourning protocol in the old way became next to impossible. It was during the First World War that the wearing of black armbands replaced everyday mourning dress for men.

After the First World War, the ritual of the Victorian funeral with horse-drawn hearse was only observed by the urban working class and royalty, and by the 1960s it had more or less died out.

Likewise for state funerals – Winston Churchill's casket travelled in a motor hearse when it wasn't on a gun carriage, or, at one point, a police launch on the river Thames.

Nowadays it's more or less only for urban working class royalty, or more precisely Cockney working class royalty: Pearly Kings and Queens.

Another branch of urban working class aristocracy that stuck with the old-fashioned funeral was also London-based. An aristocracy that ruled their manors with a fist of iron (or in Ronnie Kray's case, a hoof of iron) – the crime families of Old London Town.

"No-one locked the front door" (in the limos in the cortege)

It looks like the tradition died with Reggie Kray in 2000, because Charlie Richardson went off in a motor hearse in 2012, even if it was a vintage Rolls Royce.

One of the limos in Charlie's cortège had a floral tribute that spelled out "240DC" in white chrysanthemums.

This commemorated a WWII army generator of the type used to set off explosive charges which featured prominently in the evidence at the trial of Charles and his brother in 1966. It was apparently used to punish the taking of liberties, being attached to the victim's genitals or nipples while a charge was cranked up.

The brothers always denied using torture, but it's hard to see what the joke would have been in having a voltage-based floral tribute if that were the case. What jollity would there be to be had in celebrating a perjury that was used to fit you up for 18 years inside?

Bruce Reynolds, mastermind of the Great Train Robbery, went off in a modern hearse and a wicker coffin, and without the benefit of any mailbag or locomotive floral tributes.

His funeral's remembered more for Ronnie Biggs' response to the press photographers at what turned out to be his last public appearance – an old fashioned two-fingered 'V' sign delivered with the back of the hand outwards.

(Note to younger readers and those from outside the UK or Commonwealth: with the hand this way round, rather than 'V for Victory', this signifies 'Fuck Off'. Interestingly, there are many photographs of Winston Churchill flashing this variation, always with a cheeky grin.)

Ronnie Biggs himself, most notorious of the Great Train Robbers, went for the same modern hearse/wicker coffin combo as Bruce Reynolds, and in an even bigger departure from tradition, people were asked not to wear black, although most of them did anyway.

The coffin was draped with the Union Jack and a Brazilian flag, with an old-fashioned barber's pole Arsenal scarf and his hat laid on top, like a field marshal's uniform cap and medals. He also had a New Orleans jazz band leading the hearse, and a Hell's Angels motorcycle escort.

Rather than a cosh or a mailbag, the single floral tribute on Ronnie's hearse celebrated his farewell performance at Bruce Reynolds' funeral: a giant V sign flashed through the back window of the hearse as Ronnie's last message to the world.

Since "Mad" Frankie Fraser, in-gang electrical and dental practitioner for the Richardsons, chose the same modern Rolls-Royce hearse from the same firm as Charlie Richardson, and eschewed voltage or pliers-based floral tributes for a family-centric DAD/GRANDAD/FRANK hearsetop set, the last hope for an old-fashioned crime family horse-drawn funeral lies with Eddie Richardson, but the signs aren't good – a depressingly modern Richardson trend has been set by Charlie and Frankie.

In the United States the subject of underworld floral tributes and mourning ritual is an altogether more serious business. Most pastors in urban neighbourhoods ban the wearing of gang colours at church services, and many funeral homes likewise for floral displays.

Gang funerals often generate new business for the undertaker, as, notwithstanding any bans on gang colours, the presence of rival gang members in the congregation, all of whom carry a gun in the same way the rest of us do a handkerchief, frequently leads to the use of deadly force, as their response to an insult is just as reflexive as ours might be to a sneeze.

Mob funerals tend to be more sedate. Most mobsters are Catholic and they don't want to upset the priest and scupper the chances of their own souls' eternal rest, or less piously, expose their family to the shame of their not having a church funeral.

Rather than gang colours, it's the Armani suit and wraparound sunglasses look, but the police photographers with telephoto lenses are still very much in attendance, the long-distance lenses in this case being more to do with not causing offence, rather than avoiding stray ordnance as they are at gang banger funerals.

XIII

The Future of Undertaking

From the customer's point of view, it may well be business pretty much as usual for the immediate future. There has been talk for years about softer and cuddlier, greener, more eco-friendly, anti-corporate stirrings in the world of undertaking – new model undertakers run by women, DIY funeral companies that help the family do it their way, woodland burials, and "flameless cremation", "green cremation", "eco cremation", "bio cremation" and the like, but so far, these developments all remain alternative, not mainstream.

Perhaps surprisingly, most British undertakers are still independents, not part of a corporate chain such as Dignity or the Co-op, and perhaps even more surprisingly, it's the same in the US.

That will probably continue, because while the chains buy up independent undertakers, they also close unproductive branches down. The 'golden bricks' effect where property prices are high also makes selling or redeveloping buildings for housing attractive.

There's also the fact that more new undertakers are appearing these days – in the past, new shops tended to be expansion by existing family businesses, rather than being opened by someone who's completely new to the game.

As I've said before, the funeral trade used to be like a closed shop run by some sort of secretive mafia, and it was difficult to get a job at an undertaker's unless you'd already had one somewhere else or were related to someone who had.

The new undertakers are a new type of undertaker – younger operatives, more women, pastel colours, wicker coffins, woodland burials.

The fact that they're appearing now has more to do with a gradual breaking down of the closed-shop secrecy that used to obtain, starting with TV programmes like Six Feet Under and memoirs like The Dismal Trade, and with demands by the public that weren't being satisfied; rather than a shortage of undertakers as such.

I can say that with some certainty because now is practically the first time in history that custom is on a downturn for undertakers. It's to do with recent medical advances – which means a temporary deferral of trade, as people who should be dying now are kept alive longer – and also the hotting up of competition due to the corporate chains, but, most of all, demographics.

The future's bright

Before and during the Second World War, the birthrate fell, and that dip is working its way through the system now.

But, when the effect of the post-war baby boom starts to make itself felt in the mortality figures, undertakers should be raking it in.

Or perhaps not …

DIY

Unlike the US, you're not obliged by law to use an undertaker in the UK (and undertakers themselves have to be licensed by the state in the US).

If you look at the certificate for disposal (The Green Form) that the local Registrar of Births and Deaths gives you when you register a death (which is yellow and from the Coroner's office if there's been a post-mortem) it says you should give it to the "landowner where the burial is to take place".

In theory, that includes the Church of England – as long as you live in the parish, you're entitled to be buried in the church graveyard, even if you're not a member of the congregation.

In fact, you don't even have to be a Christian: you can conduct your own service, or use a rabbi or imam/bilal/muezzin/muzim if you want. There has to be space for a new burial plot, though, there'll probably be a big queue, and it's usually expensive – talk to the vicar in advance.

If you do it all yourself, you even sign the Burial Certificate yourself, not the vicar. You probably won't be allowed to dig the grave yourself though. Most graveyards insist on using a professional, usually their own, for health and safety reasons. They don't want to be sued if the sides of the grave you're digging collapse and bury you instead of the intended occupant.

For a municipal cemetery, you give the Green or Yellow Form to the cemetery registrar.

If you want to use a site hasn't been used for human burial before, the landowner should ask the council to come and check there's no chance of polluting a watercourse.

If you want a cremation, you'll need more bits of paper, signed by four different doctors, all of which cost money. That's because there'll be no body to dig up for tests if something suspicious about the death shows up later. Most crematoriums will be very helpful, and some even have someone whose job it is to deal with DIY customers. Again, give them as much warning as you can.

Some undertakers, and a very few wholesale coffin manufacturers, will sell you a coffin, or you can make your own – but if it's for cremation, check beforehand with the crematorium what you're allowed to make it from. There are strict rules, all to do with toxic emissions released by burning.

If you buy a coffin, it might be a good idea to warn everyone not to use the handles for carrying, because they're sometimes more ornamental than functional.

Some undertakers will hire you a hearse and driver, or you can use an estate car or van, or carry the coffin yourselves if it's not too far. Four bearers are better than six: with six you'll only get in each other's way.

Remember to set off walking in step, or the coffin will bounce up and down on your shoulders, and take some trestles with you so you can have rests or change bearers.

Funeral processions in rural Ireland involve the entire village, and they still walk the whole route to the church.

Carrying the coffin is considered an honour, and is taken in turn.
These traditions were followed by the London Irish into the 1970s, and the route to the church could cover several miles if someone died in south London and the family church was in north London. The procession would stop at every pub on the way, while the coffin was left outside on trestles.

Dead Reckoning

The wholesale cost of a coffin, and the undertaker's mark-up on the price to you, is frequently advanced to support the idea that undertakers are all unprincipled conmen who take advantage of vulnerable people in their hour of grief.

I believe the wholesale price of a coffin hasn't changed much in twenty years: about sixty quid. The undertaker might seal the inside with a bitumen mixture called coffin compound, then he lines it with the stuff disposable nappies are made of, trims it with foam-backed polyester and lace using dome-headed upholstery tacks, and puts the coffin furniture on – nameplate and handles. They used to french polish the outside in the old days, but it's all veneers (plastic or wood) and polyester resin finishes now.

Incidentally, if you've paid top dollar for solid oak or elm, or whatever wood it might be, check the baseboard. That's the most expensive piece of wood, and unscrupulous undertakers sometimes use chipboard for this bit, because no-one ever sees it, and the only people who might notice are the bearers, and they're usually undertaker's men anyway.

If they're not, no-one's going to stop the proceedings to start peering under the coffin, and if they did, 1. it would look bloody odd, and, 2. it would be too late anyway:

"Hey, hold on, this isn't solid oak! Come on, get it back in the hearse. Sorry everyone, but there's not going to be any funeral until this has been put right."

Chipboard is 'particleboard' in the US, but wooden coffins are uncommon there. They like metal caskets with rubber gaskets, using the same kind of technology and finish as car doors.

After trimming and finishing it, the undertaker could charge you at least six or seven times what he paid for the coffin. You might think that's shocking, but is it really?
What does a carrot cost, and how much does it cost to put it on your plate in a posh restaurant? How much do you then pay for it?

If you manage to find a manufacturer who will sell a coffin to you, it won't cost a lot less than it would from an undertaker – and why should it? Retail customers don't get wholesale prices in other businesses. Wicker coffins and cardboard coffins can cost about the same as a cheap wooden coffin, too, although you should be able to get a cardboard one for a lot less if you shop around.

But zeroing in on the cost of a coffin misses the point. Undertaking is a service industry, not product retailing. Undertaking is a specialised branch of event management, and the charges compare pretty well with those of a wedding organiser, for instance, for what is in many ways a similar event (except for the fact that there are two bodies involved, and while they might go somewhere hot afterwards, they don't come back in an urn).

When you've got to go...Go Green

The other developments in the world of undertaking for which much is promised are in the 'flameless cremation' area. Most of these silly-sounding euphemisms – "liquid" or "bio" cremation and the like – are based on a process called alkaline hydrolysis as a means to reduce the corpse to its chemical components, with that process itself euphemised as "tissue reduction" or "water reduction".

Promession, Cryomation and Ecolation use cryogenic freezing.

What's so wrong with burial and cremation that we need a new method after all these years (about 100,000 years, actually, from around when our ancestors were still rubbing shoulders with Neanderthals)?

There are just too many of us.

Space is the big problem with burial. As the city churchyards became literally full to overflowing (with ground level in the churchyard seven or eight feet above street level), new parkland cemeteries like Père Lachaise in Paris (1804), followed by Manchester, Liverpool and London were opened, but this could only be a stopgap solution, as cities spread and land values rose.

Cremation began to be promoted on grounds of hygiene and space-saving, and the first crematoria in Britain and the US opened in the late 1880s as the practice was approved by the Church.

Cremation has been legal in Britain since 1884, as the result of a court case involving yet another of the eccentric doctors who seem to crop up so frequently in the history of funerals and undertaking.

Or, more accurately, the fact that it wasn't illegal was confirmed.

Dr William Price of Llantrisant was a follower of Iolo Morganwg (Edward Wiliams, aka 'Ned of Glamorgan'), a poet, forger and inventor of 'ancient' Druidic tradition (along the same lines as James MacPherson with his 'Celtic' sagas of Ossian and bogus Scottish tradition). Part of the mumbo-jumbo that Williams came up with was an idea that burial is unclean, and the ancient British way was cremation. (He was, however, also a poet of some talent, and we have him to thank for the Eisteddfodd and the modern Welsh Bardic tradition.)

While Dr Price followed Williams' neo-Druidism, he followed no-one when it came to fashion, being almost as singular in that respect as Dr Martin van Butchell, the man who had his wife embalmed as a household ornament. Like van Butchell, he didn't believe in barbers, ending up with a waist-length beard and shoulder-length hair that he wore in plaits.

Price never wore socks, which he thought were unhygienic, and often nothing else either. He found he composed his best poetry when he helped the process along with a combination of nudism and hill-walking.

When he did wear clothes, his outfit usually consisted of a green coat and trousers with a red waistcoat – he may have invented the concept of the suit, because the idea of wearing a jacket and pants of the same cloth was almost unknown until the late 19th century.

He also invented the Davy Crockett hat before Davy Crockett, but foxes being native to Wales rather than racoons, his was fox skin, with the fox's mask on top with the eyes peering out over his own, and the brush hanging down at the back. As time went on he added extra brushes, ending up with three.

Sometimes he liked to make more of an effort sartorially; for Druidic assemblies generally favouring the white robes that Williams/Morganwg prescribed, with a red shirt and trousers underneath.

But even more startling than his anticipation of the 20th century men's lounge suit was his demonstration of the defining features of 20th century comic book characters – fifty years before Superman made his appearance in the pages of DC comics.

At the opening of an art exhibition in Cardiff in 1884 (there weren't any phone booths then), he stripped off to reveal a form-fitting red suit covered with the letters of the alphabet in green, almost a colour negative version of Batman's arch-nemesis, The Riddler.

All men are cremated equal

Dr Price was also ahead of his time in his espousal of a British proto-socialist movement called Chartism, a cross between the first stirrings of political trade unionism and a move to extend the vote to the working class.

He also seemed to have had a suitably Marxist dislike of industrialised wage-slavery, and apparently of filthy lucre in general: he only accepted payment from poor patients if his treatment worked, and he washed every coin he was given.

He was also a vegetarian on moral grounds – "meat brings out the beast in man" – and advocated and practised free love.

Practised long and hard, which brings us to how he came to establish legal precedent on cremation in Britain.

When he was 83, his housekeeper (who was 60 years his junior) bore him a son who he named Iesu Grist – Jesus Christ in Welsh. He believed Iesu would be the new Druidic messiah, but Iesu died when he was five months old.

The neighbours were outraged when they came out of chapel and found Dr Price cremating his son in a barrel of paraffin. They intervened physically, wresting the tiny body away from the doctor after putting out the fire, and the local constabulary were forced to intervene to protect the doctor and prevent his home being destroyed in a riot. They also confiscated the body and arrested Price.

This wasn't the first time Price had come to the attention of the authorities – he had to leave on the first boat to France from Liverpool following his involvement in the Welsh Chartist uprising of 1839, not returning until the heat died down some years later.

It must surely be a tribute to his personal authority or skill as a doctor, or both, that his devoutly religious neighbours in an area still famous for its uncompromising interpretation of the gospel hadn't laid hands on him before, given the provocation his religious, political and sexual activities must have been to them.

By all accounts he was a compelling public speaker, a talent which he exercised not only in what Marx (whom he supposedly met while he was in France) would have called the Chartist militant tendency, but also in yet another years-before-his-time enthusiasm of his: recreational litigation.

He mostly appeared in the small claims court, usually over unpaid bills and alleged slurs or impugning of his reputation.

At the hearing for the case concerning the cremation of his son, he argued that cremation was legal because there was no mention in British law of it being illegal. The judge agreed with Price, ruling that cremation was not illegal so long as it didn't constitute a public nuisance, and since Price had been attempting to cremate his son on his own land, he was not guilty.

Price then reclaimed the body of his son and completed the cremation. His own, in 1893, on the same hill on the edge of the town, drew a crowd of 20,000, and was the first legally-sanctioned public cremation in Britain.

But, as we have seen, people are very conservative when it comes to death and funerals, and despite Dr Price's early espousal, cremation only overtook burial as the number one choice in Britain in 1967, and they're only just catching up in America now (estimated at 48.2% in 2015, from only 3.5% in 1960); perhaps because space for burial hasn't been a historical problem over there.

The problem with cremation is that, while it solves the graveyard sprawl problem; with the kind of numbers involved today, the air pollution gets serious, and not just in terms of greenhouse gas emissions.

60% of the mercury pollution in the UK is from amalgam in tooth fillings vapourised and released into the atmosphere by cremation. It can be filtered out, but upgrading one crematorium costs £1.2 million. New crematoria are correspondingly more expensive.

One problem that can't be got round is the amount of energy cremation uses. The retort has to be heated to 1100°C, and then kept there – heating and cooling is what destroys the lining of the retort, which is expensive to replace, so it's kept hot for as long as possible once it's been fired up.

But, while you can't exactly avoid the problem of high energy use, there are ways to get more bang for your bucks.

Waste not, want not

They use heat from cremation for the municipal hot water system in Halmstad in Sweden, and to heat a school at Byskov, near Copenhagen. The perfect solution would be a dual use municipal crematorium and waste incinerator plumbed into the communal hot water supply, a technically elegant disposal solution which even the rationalist Scandis probably aren't ready for yet.

But however efficiently you might wring the most out of every last therm used for cremation, and however painstakingly you might filter out the heavy metal pollution, the problem of CO^2 emissions will still remain. Until carbon capture (storing carbon dioxide underground) becomes more than just a clever idea, the CO^2 is a problem that's going to get bigger and bigger, just when we should be cutting it down.

So what about the 21st century improvements on cremation? Despite being around since the 20th century, most of them are still ideas waiting to take off, or even happen at all.

I'll start with Promession, not because it's the best, and certainly not because it's the most successful, but because it's the one you're most likely to have heard about. That may be not unconnected with the fact that its inventor has been accused of being better at publicity than the science involved.

Susanne Wiihg-Mäsak is a former marine biologist who has worked as a technician at a petro-chemical company and now runs a market-gardening business on a small island north of Gothenburg.

She's always been big on composting, and apparently even gives courses on it. That's what Promession is all about, with a sprinkling of sci-fi space technology, and a biodegradable coffin instead of a compost bin propped up on bricks at the bottom of the garden.

The advantages of Promession (and its rivals, which I will come to) are that you end up with compostable remains that fit in a box a third the size of a normal coffin, and help save the earth from global warming.

In a normal burial, you have to bury the body deep, because being in one large piece means that it gets degraded from the inside out, by anaerobic bacteria. They don't need oxygen, but unfortunately they make methane, a greenhouse gas that's worse than carbon dioxide.

With Promession, the remains are degraded by aerobic bacteria, just like compost, and they can be buried in a much shallower grave.

Why is it called Promession? Like some other things about it, the name doesn't quite seem to make sense. Like me, you may have thought it suggests something, or has some kind of appropriate associations, in a Scandinavian language.

Not at all, it's called that because it's the Italian for "promise".

No wiser? Well, it's all about promising to return to the earth what emerged from the earth (both facts according to an interview with Wiigh-Mäsak in the Daily Telegraph).
Still doesn't quite stack up for me. Surely it's plants that emerge from the earth? In the animal kingdom we tend to do our emerging from our actual mothers rather than mother earth.

And if things don't quite seem to stack up with regard to the name, there's been some suggestion that they don't stack up in terms of how Promession is supposed to work, either. Not the basics – they've been around since a retired science teacher from Eugene, Oregon called Phillip Backman patented them in 1978.

First of all, you chill the body down to -18°C, then you stick it in a vat of liquid nitrogen. That makes it very brittle, so brittle that if you give it a good tap, it shatters. You may well have seen this demonstrated on science programmes on TV, where they usually like to do this with a flower.

The problem is, a human cadaver is a lot bigger than a flower, and it contains bones, some of them quite big, amongst other things not found in flowers; so it doesn't shatter into small pieces in the same way. Mr Backman's patent suggests using something that works along the same principles as a hammer mill at this point.

The same problem with bones comes up in cremation. One solution used there is the cremulator, something like a tumble dryer with big ball bearings in it (but without the hot air blower, obviously).

Human bones are made of tough stuff, tough enough to stand 70 minutes at 1100°C. They're about all that is left after cremation – as I've said before, there's no need to worry about getting ash from the coffin mixed in with your mum's ashes: what you get in the urn (or cardboard box from some of the stingier councils) is just bone ash, and it is just your mother's bone ash. Despite what you may have heard, only one body at a time is cremated.

(By the way, you will read over and over again on the internet that a human cremation takes between two and three hours. In a modern municipal crematorium the body of an average-sized man takes around 70 minutes, taking longer depending on the size of the body, and only rarely more than two, or at the most three hours. I think the two to three hours relates to the kind of equipment found in American funeral homes.)

In Promession, the problem of reducing bone is apparently accomplished by ultrasound or vibration, or a combination of the two.

No-one's quite sure, because Ms Wiihg-Mäsak isn't too clear on this point, and although the process has apparently been applied to pig carcasses, it seems that's only been demonstrated before invited audiences, not at a public press or media event, or, despite requests, to satisfy sceptics of the process.

When Promession first appeared, I remember only ultrasound was mentioned as a reducing agent, which sounded a bit too space-age and science-fictioney to be true. Ultrasound is used to clean museum specimens like old coins, and for non-destructive testing of machine parts and welds. The only application remotely similar to this is breaking up gall- and kidney stones, but they're tiny, and nothing like as tough as bone.

One sceptic who's gone public with his misgivings about Promession is Bengt Johansson, professor in cellular biology and medicine at Gothenburg University. He said that it's all a big bluff, and that it can't work as described because human bones are too tough to reduce without some mechanical treatment. And apparently fat and skin are even tougher when frozen, and there's more of them to deal with.

Surely the best way to shut him and the other critics up would be to invite them to a demonstration of Promession?

When this point is put to her, Ms Wiigh-Märsak says she doesn't want to give away the secrets of the process to her competitors. She also says that the opposition to Promession is orchestrated by powerful forces in the cremation industry.

That's as may be, but I think the most telling charge against Promession is the fact that the UK franchise announced in 2012 that they were severing all ties with Promessa Organic AB (Sweden), and that "after a lengthy period of due diligence Promessa UK believes that Promession is still at concept stage".

If people who actually bought into it decided it was still at the concept stage 15 years after Susanne Wiigh-Mäsak started out with it, it's a pretty damning indictment.

In 2012 the Swedish government ordered that the bodies of nine people who'd signed up for Promession and were being kept in cold storage were to be cremated or buried.

Cryomation

Cryomation is a kind of Scottish version of Promession, with all the eco credentials, but without the red herring of ultrasound. The fragments left after freezing are reduced mechanically, and the patent also includes an autoclave cycle to sterilise the remains.

Yes, contrary to what may seem a reasonable assumption, freezing with liquid nitrogen doesn't kill bacteria (or prions, which cause things like Mad Cow disease) – it preserves them.
Which isn't so surprising if you remember that this is actually just freeze-drying, which is normally used to preserve food, tissue samples and sperm.

The most recent addition in the nitrogen-cooled line-up is a very new contender from Ireland:

Ecolation (no, not ecolocation, that's how bats find their way around).

Where the other two use a bath of liquid nitrogen to freeze the body, Ecolation uses a stream of "cryogenic gaseous nitrogen" only slightly warmer than liquid nitrogen, but apparently quicker-acting and cheaper. The pressure and temperature difference also make it a lot easier and cheaper to transport and store.

"Pressure waves" from multiple blasts of high-pressure air are then used to break up the remains. That might sound a bit like another ultrasound-type fudge to avoid the bad PR associations of harsh-sounding mechanical methods, but it seems the Ecolation process has been tested from start to finish and proved to work.

It successfully reduced a 100kg pig called Muriel to 1.3kg of black granules similar in texture and consistency to instant coffee.

Cryomation's end product is grey, there's more of it, and it's compostable in the same way as Promession's. That's because Cryomation uses conventional methods to dry the remains after they've been reduced to fragments. We're made of something like 60% water, and if that wasn't extracted at some point, you'd be left with a heavy, moist, mulch-type material that might start composting a bit too soon.

I've been told by the company CEO that Ecolation dries and sterilizes the remains by using "a physical process that changes long chain molecules into short chain molecules in a dry environment", in the same way as which gas and oil are produced when plants in sediments are turned into fossils.

I believe the process involved there is pyrolysis, a chemical reaction which involves high temperatures in a closed environment with no oxygen present. The nitrofreezing and pneumatic blasts must in effect serve to reduce the body to small enough pieces for pyrolysis to work efficiently. If the fragments weren't small enough, they'd end up just being charred on the outside.

All these methods use less energy than cremation, and produce less pollution (no mercury, because you simply sift out the tooth fillings). The nitrogen they use is more or less a byproduct from liquid oxygen production.

With Ecolation, you're left with something that could be scattered like ashes, and with burial following Cryomation the intention is to recycle the grave plot, with either no memorial, something temporary perhaps made of wood, or a shrub or a tree planted on the grave (which could of course leave the same problem with space as conventional burial if the tree isn't cut down fairly soon).

For any of them to be used by the funeral industry, they have to be covered by government regulation. So far only South Korea has enacted specific legislation, for Promession.

The Solution Solution

Unlike the nitro-freeze techniques, the other alternative to cremation and burial is already in use.

Alkaline hydrolysis has been used to dispose of animal remains for some years, likewise for human body parts at hospitals, and is licensed for the disposal of human bodies in parts of the US & Canada, Asia and Australia.

Once again, as with so many other innovations in the funeral world –Drs van Butchell, Hunter and Johnston with modern embalming, Dr Price with modern cremation, crape, royal effigies, department stores of death, feather farming, artificial jet, the black armband – I'm proud to be able to hail alkaline hydrolysis as yet another Great British invention.

The process was first patented by Amos Herbert Hobson of Westminster, London at the US patent office on the 5th of April 1888.

He didn't patent it with the funeral trade in mind, though, more as a means of extracting gelatin or glue from animal bones, with the added benefit that what was left made good fertiliser.

It wasn't until 1994 that the first patent concerning the disposal of bodies (animal and human) was filed, again at the USPO, from that other rich source of innovation for the world of undertaking, the medical profession (vide Drs van Butchell, Hunter – both of them, Johnston, Price, Holmes, Gannal, Souquet and von Hagens).

Gordon Kaye was a professor of pathology who was looking for a safe way to dispose of lab animals who had been used in experiments involving radioactive isotopes at Albany Medical College NY, and Peter Weber was his counterpart at the biochemistry department who suggested alkaline hydrolysis.

So good they named it twice...

They formed a company called Waste Reduction by Waste Reduction Inc., or WR^2, which was mainly concerned with processing animal remains but later expanded to human application.

...but even so, not, for some reason, part of the Sinatra back catalogue

A body in a silk bag is boiled in a hot caustic solution in a big pressure cooker. The hydrogen ions from the water in the body combine with the molecules of the solution, neutralising its alkalinity and in the process breaking up the fat and protein molecules of the body, leaving a bag of bones and mercury fillings, pacemakers, artificial hips etc, and a runoff of pH neutral, sterile liquid.

In disposing of animal carcasses, the wastewater is used to make fertiliser or to manufacture biogas for electricity generation, but with humans it just goes down the drain. The bones that are left genuinely do crumble at the lightest touch, so there's no mechanical reduction, ultrasound or pressure waves involved.

The main suppliers of alkaline hydrolysis machines to the funeral trade are Aquamation of Australia and Resomation of Scotland.

"*Resomation*"? We're back to foreign languages again, this time classical – resoma is the Greek for rebirth (don't blame me if that's not right, it's from their website).

A bit of an odd choice for a name, given that this is about reducing dead bodies to a heap of sterile powder, but they don't call it that in America, where all the customers are so far.

No, they call it 'Biocremation' or 'Flameless Cremation' over there.

There are two reasons for that.

First of all, PR: it relates this newcomer to the funeral business to something familiar, plus, you can make out it's 'gentler' or 'less harsh' because it 'involves water, not flames'.

But the main reason is to get round having to pass new laws.

Cremation is already licensed for the disposal of human remains in all US states, as is, similarly, alkaline hydrolysis for the disposal of animal remains for the livestock and food processing industries.

There is also pre-existing legislation allowing the use of alkaline hydrolysis on human remains in hospitals and medical schools in some states – the first ever alkaline hydrolysis of a whole human body was in 2006, at the Mayo Clinic, Minnesota, using a WR^2 machine.

Classifying alkaline hydrolysis machinery as cremation equipment means its use is covered by existing legislation, avoiding the need for ill-informed argy-bargy in the state legislature about, for instance, the 'disrespect' of disposing of the wastewater in the public drainage system, or ignorant suggestions of possible danger of infection, as has happened.

How is this any more 'disrespectful' than washing blood and body fluids from embalming or surgery down the drain?
There was a problem with the run-off being slightly viscous and possibly clogging pipes with the sodium hydroxide that was used originally, but that was fixed by switching to potassium hydroxide.

And there's no danger of infection, because the process of alkaline hydrolysis renders both the run-off and the remains completely sterile.

That's why it was already licensed for the cattle industry – it's the only method apart from incineration that guarantees the destruction of prions.

As land-use pressures begin to apply in the US regarding burial, and as the problems of controlling CO^2 emissions and energy use grow regarding cremation, alkaline hydrolysis will probably become more popular.

It's also cheaper, claimed to be variously a tenth or a seventh of the cost of cremation (oddly enough, the price to the customer isn't a tenth of the cost of cremation, though – it usually works out to be about the same when all the extras have been included).

The only problem from the operator's view is that at two and a half to four hours, it will usually take longer than cremation, but if the operator is a funeral home in the US, then it doesn't take a lot longer – as I've already pointed out, the plant they use is slower than that at municipal crematoria.

Aquamation

Aquamation Industries operates in Australia, the US and Canada. The first alkaline hydrolysis by the funeral trade worldwide was an Aquamation in Australia in 2010, and also the first in America, in January 2011.

Unlike Resomation, Aquamation is an NPLT system – No Pressure Low Temperature – which means it takes quite a bit longer, but which also means it uses less energy, and therefore costs less. It also means an aperture can be left at the top of the machine through which the soul can migrate, an important consideration, apparently, for potential customers in SE Asia.

Funeral trade use of alkaline hydrolysis is growing, with the number of procedures performed worldwide now into four figures.

But not, so far, in Britain. Which is odd, because in theory, getting legislative approval here should be easier than under federal systems like the US, Canada or Australia.

Rather than arguing the case in the legislative assemblies of every unitary regional authority up and down the country, it's just up to the Ministry of Justice, and their main concern would be the same as with cremation – the fact that there's no body to dig up and examine if suspicions are raised afterwards.

You might wonder why the procedures already in place for cremation can't be used.

And you might also imagine that, because alkaline hydrolysis has been used here by the livestock and food processing industries for some time, the environmental and public health aspects are already looked after, so there shouldn't be any problem with the Department of the Environment, Food and Rural Affairs.

It's because the authorities here won't extend the regulation of cremation to include alkaline hydrolysis as a new kind of 'flameless cremation', as in the US.

According to the Cremation Society Annual Reports 2011/12 (yes, perhaps surprisingly, they're fans of

Resomation), the previous (Labour) government decided that alkaline hydrolysis "does not constitute the burning of human remains and therefore falls outside the current regulatory framework" and that there should be a full public consultation on alternatives to cremation. The incoming Coalition put that idea on the back burner (no pun intended), and no-one's touched it since.

With Ecolation, however, it could be argued that the key part of the process, pyrolysis, is, quite literally, flameless cremation, and is therefore covered by current regulatory framework. The same logic would apply in America, or anywhere else, with better justification than in the case of alkaline hydrolysis.

In any case, given the problems of pollution and energy use with cremation, and of space with burial, it seems inevitable that the future of undertaking will see both of those age-old practices overtaken by something greener and more sustainable.

All the above contenders represent big improvements on cremation in terms of sustainability and damage to the environment, but which is best?

The Ecology of Death

The only large-scale comparative study so far was commissioned by a Dutch funeral company from TNO, The Netherlands Organisation for Applied Scientific Research, an independent statutory body that does research for industry and government.

It was produced as a first step in amending the law to allow Resomation and Cryomation in the Netherlands (Ecolation had yet to be invented).

It's certainly thorough, at 88 pages, and the first surprise is that, even though they didn't evaluate it fully, the environmental cost of pre-disposal procedures – transport, refrigeration and storage of the body, sending out of invitations, travel to 'farewell ceremony', use of assembly space for 'farewell ceremony', etc – was found to be larger than that of the 'disposal procedure' itself.

Perhaps we need to go back to carrying the coffin ourselves and walking to the funeral.

They used *Life Cycle Analysis* to assess the different methods. LCA is also, appropriately in this case, known as 'cradle to grave' analysis – the idea is to include every effect on the environment throughout the whole 'life cycle' of everything involved – production of raw materials, transport, manufacture, disposal.

Burial comes out worst, then cremation, and Cryomation and Resomation come in way ahead, almost neck and neck. However, when the Shadow Price is taken into account, quote: "the impact of resomation is (probably) lowest of all funeral options."

The *Shadow Price* is what society is willing to pay to reduce emissions to meet environmental targets. Breaking those figures down, Cryomation and Resomation compare pretty well with each other on everything except *HTP*.

Human Toxicity Potential is the harm toxins released into the environment could do to people. The HTP cost for Cryomation is less than zero, but that's still beaten by Resomation with an incredible minus 7€.

(We can assume Ecolation would also have also gotten a minus score here, because of the effects of pyrolation.)

The other difference is *Eutrophication* – algal blooms in rivers and lakes, something usually caused by fertiliser run off from farmer's fields or leaks from their slurry tanks. It's serious because the algae use all the oxygen in the water, and that kills everything else.

In this department, Resomation loses out to Cryomation (as it would to Ecolation, if it had been included.)

So, it looks to be pretty cut and dried, then. All the new high-tech methods come out way ahead of burial and cremation in ecological terms.

Except it's not. One of the main reasons burial came off so badly in this study is the use of gravestones and their associated environmental costs.

The stone mostly comes all the way from China these days, because they can quarry it and work it for less there and the costs of shipping things in bulk carriers are lower than they ever have been, now that bulk carriers are so big.

So, making gravestones from Chinese stone is low in price; but high in environmental costs.

The other problem with gravestones that skews the results against burial is land use. As long as a gravestone's on top of it, that bit of land can't be re-used.

Then there's the fact that all the carbon miles and costs of manufacture invested in the coffin get buried with it – with the other methods (and Ecolation) the coffin gets re-used. The calculations are for an 'average' wooden coffin, and assumes use of a grave for 35 years before bones are removed and the site can be re-used (Dutch graves are rented out leasehold, ten years at a time).

It's worse in Britain, where it usually takes at least 75 years before a grave gets re-used.

Green burial avoids all these ecoproblems of course, but green burial was until recently almost unknown in the Netherlands, so this study doesn't take it into account.

If it had been included, it would surely have been the winner – no energy used to process the body, biodegradable coffin, and because the burial isn't too deep, low-to-no methane emissions.

Britain is, once again, something of a world leader here (I know, this is getting monotonous, but it's true). There are more green burial sites here than any other country – not per head of population, more actual sites. Astounding if you compare the population of Britain to, say, the US. No official statistics are kept, but it's been estimated that there are over 10,000 green burials a year in the UK.

The trouble is, with nearly 500,000 deaths a year, if everyone opted for a green burial, space would be a problem, even with recycling of plots.

In its purest form, green burial means no fixed memorial of any kind, but marking a grave so that you have something to visit is a very strong human impulse. A marker made of wood, say, for a limited period wouldn't be much of problem, but planting trees or shrubs could become one, if they weren't removed. (With woodland burial, the idea is to turn the land back to forest, of course.)

9,600 new green burials every week would saturate the existing sites in Britain within a year or two, and finding enough suitable sites close to towns and cities might not be so easy. It would mean turning farmland over to green burial. It's all possible, of course, but I suspect there might have to be some kind of government policy to promote or legislate to get everyone doing it.

Urban Death Project of Seattle (founder, director and sole employee as of 2015, Katrina Spade) proposes industrialising green burial for urban areas by having it happen in a kind of neighbourhood composting factory, with the communal compost produced being available to everyone for gardening or whatever they wanted to use it for. Don't hold your breath for this one though, it probably won't be going anywhere in a hurry.
1. There would have to be an awful lot of factories, 2. the assembly line would be very slow (bones again), and 3, the clincher: despite UDP's claims, the 140C that can be generated in composting will not destroy pathogens like prions.

There would also be a powerful NIMBY effect – most people wouldn't be too keen on the idea of an industrial (dis)assembly line for corpses as a next door neighbour, even if it did mean, on the bonus side, all the compost your window box could ever need.

A drop in the ocean

The problem of the sheer numbers involved would also apply in the case of the other green method, burial at sea. There are only three areas in UK waters where you can do it, because of the chances of the bodies turning up on the beach or in fishermen's nets.

You have to get a permit from the Marine Management Organisation. It's also very expensive – you'll need to hire a boat from the nearest ports on the Isle of Wight, at Tynemouth, or from Hastings or Newhaven, and transport the body there. You're not allowed to embalm the body either, so there could be storage problems if you can't arrange everything quickly enough.

It's easier in the US, but you'll still need a permit from your city or local authority and you need to inform the Environmental Protection Agency. You have to go at least three nautical miles offshore, and the water has to be deep enough – that means 75 miles out from New York, for instance, but only five from Miami. The distance on the west coast is usually only three miles.

Around the rest of the world, it's usually only permitted if the deceased had 'strong maritime connections', such as a long-serving maritime career, as in Australia.

Over my dead body!

I'm often told that the biggest problem with all the new methods is public perception, or what we might call the PR factor.

Perhaps it might be better to call it the Yeuch! factor, since it concerns the illogical yet apparently instinctive tendency in some people to dwell on the physical details of disposing of a dead body, as though they would be happening to a living, breathing mother, grandfather or whoever, rather than a dead body.

Promoters of the different new methods like to play up the yeuch factors of their opponent's methods:

"Alkaline hydrolysis will never catch on, people don't want to think of their loved ones being washed down the drain."
or
"Cryogenic freezing is just high-tech window-dressing to disguise the fact that the body has to be minced up into little pieces to make compost – they might just as well use a log chipper."

But if you applied that attitude to burial or cremation, they'd sound as if they had even less going for them.

It took a long time for cremation to catch on, but it did, and in the end that probably had more to do with an increasing disparity between the cost of cremation and burial than any shift in sensibilities.

So, maybe rather than the problem being 'public perception' of the new methods, that's just 'perception of public perception', and the real problem is relative cost – if the old methods get expensive enough, and the new methods are sufficiently cheaper, people will suddenly find themselves able to overcome their misgivings and just get on with it.

Cemetery burial is already pricing itself out of most people's consideration, and a carbon tax would have the same effect on cremation.

This is a problem with global financial implications, serving a multibillion dollar industry – the UK funeral industry is worth £1 billion annually, and the US $20 billion (£11 billion) – but the question of what will replace cremation and burial has so far escaped serious consideration in the media.

Green burial might be the most ecological answer, but apart from questions of whether there's enough space for it if people can't be weaned off gravestones, it's less attractive to big business because they can't make money out of it in the same way as building and selling or licensing technology, the familiar ways of doing business.

But even so, big business has started to take an interest in green burial nonetheless, and instead of dealing with idealists and green-minded farmers or landowners, you could find yourself paying over the odds to subsidise executive bonuses and shareholders' dividends.

A plot usually costs something like £500, but some of the corporate-run sites that some undertakers might point you towards are now charging £700 or more.

More public perception

This is an interesting time to be writing a book like this. At the beginning of it, I spoke about the changes in attitudes to death, from its inclusion as part of life, and the Victorian celebration of death, to the modern out-of-sight-out-of-mind mindset.

More recently, and even while I've been writing, there has started to be more openness about death and how we, or rather undertakers, deal with it – more newspaper articles and books like The Dismal Trade and Stiffs reviewed in the Sunday papers, fly on the wall TV programmes about undertakers, and the appearance of websites like comparethecoffin.com, goodfuneralguide.-

co.uk and naturaldeath.org (all three highly recommended, by the way, as is The Undertaking: Life Studies from the Dismal Trade, by Thomas Lynch, to give it its full title).

We've moved on from the Jekyll or Hyde presentation of undertakers that used to obtain, too. (Jessica Mitford's The American Way of Death: Undertakers Bad, versus Don't Drop the Coffin by Barry Albin-Dyer, or any other book by an undertaker: Undertakers Good.)

Like most things in life, it's a bit more complicated than that, whatever 'that' might be, in any given context.

Alongside crude hatchet jobs like Undercover Undertaker, Channel 4's sensationalist hidden camera "exposé" of "shocking" practices by the Coop, with its manufactured outrage at facts like: the Coop trades in competition with other large companies and therefore tries to maximise profit by selling more rather than less, or: bodies are "stacked up" in an "industrial building" – or, in other words, kept in a mortuary; we have also seen more nuanced programmes like Dead Good Job on BBC2, which was a fair-minded study of different funeral businesses around the UK, plus things like a biker priest with his own sidecar hearse and a terminally ill mother who arranged her own funeral.

And these are interesting times for the trade, too. Squeezed for profits by increasing crematorium and burial fees and higher certification charges and competition from green undertakers and DIY funerals, just as their role is being questioned as never before and they're being treated like mere event organisers.

As for undertakers being treated like wedding or party organisers by people who have their own ideas about what they want – a pink hearse, as it may be, or a coffin that looks like cake packaging – the same thing is happening to the funeral service and the priest.

What used to be a tightly-prescribed church ritual, the Service of Committal, the point of which was religious – to commit the soul of the deceased to God's care, with readings from an official order of service and perhaps one hymn selected from Hymns Ancient and Modern – has become a congregation-steered free-for-all where the priest goes through a biography that covers schooling, employment history, house moves, pets owned and anything else they're told to include, all, usually for someone they've never met or heard of before the undertaker gave them the gig.

The priest may well then step down and hand over the pulpit for contributions from the mourners – poetry readings, personal reminiscences or humorous stories not so far removed from the best man's speech at a wedding.

And in the crematorium chapel, typically, I Did It My Way over the PA.

I suspect there's two influences at work here – one being the effect celebrity and reality TV culture has had on people's attitudes by dissolving the barriers between public and private. People are less inclined to formality and no longer regard 'making a show of themselves' as something shameful – in fact that very concept is now just a left-over from pre-reality-TV times.

The other is changed attitudes to the clergy. Most people only have to do with a priest before and at their wedding, and more rarely, their children's christenings, and for funerals.

The attitude is, "I'm paying, and it's costing enough, so you'll do as I say".

The old-fashioned view (or strictly accurate view, if you take a reductionist stance) is that this is a church service, for the soul of the deceased, and that type of thing belongs at a memorial service or the wake.

I'm not taking sides – as far as I'm concerned, the funeral ceremony is for the mourners, not the deceased, and they should have whatever comforts them. It seems a bit odd, though, if you want a Christian burial/cremation service, to insist on making it up yourself. If you don't want a religious service, why drag a priest into it?

Famous last words

And finally... how would I like my own remains to be disposed of?

The favourite would be donating my body to medical science. There's a shortage of bodies for British medical students to learn anatomy from, largely due to an outbreak of superstition and prejudice fuelled by the way British tabloids whip up scandal and hysteria using sad incidents like the pathologist at Alder Hey hospital who took babies' organs for specimens without asking the parents. (Don't worry, that case was a one-off then, and since then the Human Tissue Authority has been set up specifically to stop things like that ever happening again.)

The fallout from this sensationalist reporting means that more medical students have to share bodies for dissection – it used to be two students per body, but the current shortage means six students now share one body.

Another advantage of donation to science is that after it's helped some students become doctors, the hospital returns your body and pays for the funeral. At that point I suppose I would go for whichever is the winner from the current crop of replacements for cremation, or if there's a choice, the one with the smallest eco-footprint.

Although, having said that, part of me does hanker after the idea of a horse-drawn hearse, and going in a traditional lead shell in an oak casket in the vaults at my favourite cemetery, Kensal Green in London...

Bibliography

Alberti, S.J. (2011). *Morbid Curiosities. Medical Museums in Nineteenth Century Britain* Oxford: Oxford University Press

Aufderheide, A.C. (2003). *The Scientific Study of Mummies* Cambridge: Cambridge University Press

Baden, M. (1989). *Unnatural Death. Confessions of a Forensic Pathologist* New York: Ballantine

Barley, N (1995). *Dancing on the Grave. Encounters with Death* London: John Murray

Cottrell, L. (1955). *Life Under the Pharoahs* London: Pan

Cunnington, P & Lucas, C (1972). *Costumes for Births, Marriages and Deaths* London: A & C Black

Curl, J. S. (1972). *The Victorian Celebration of Death.* Newton Abbot UK: David & Charles

Dunand & Lichtenberg (1994). *Mummies A Journey Through Eternity* London: Thames & Hudson

Francis, Kellaher & Neophytu (2005). *The Secret Cemetery* Oxford, NY: Berg

Giesey, R.E. (1987). *Funeral Effigies as Emblems of Sovereignty: Europe, 14th to 18th Centuries* Paper, 6.7.87 Collège de France

Keijzer, E.E & Kok, H.J.G. (2011). *Environmental impact of different funeral technologies* Utrecht: TNO (Netherlands Organisation for Applied Scientific Research)

von Hagens & Whalley (2001). *Körperwelten – Fascination Beneath the Surface* Heidelberg: Institute for Plastination

Laufer, B (1926). *Ostrich Egg-shell Cups of Mesopotamia and the Ostrich in Ancient and Modern Times* Chicago: Field Museum anthropology leaflet 23

Litten, J. (1991). *The English Way of Death. The Common Funeral Since 1450* London: Robert Hale

Mosca, A.K. (2001). *The Enduring Legacy of Eva Peron*: Wall, NJ USA: Kates-Boylston Publications Inc.

Murcott, A. (2002). *Shouldering the Burden. Healthwork in the Locality: the Case of the Funeral Director* Paper in *Gender, Health and Healing: the Public/Private Divide* eds. Bendelow, G et al. London: Routledge

Pallarols, J.C. Unattributed biography quoted on *Official Eva Peron Website* www.evitaperon.org 2010

Pettigrew, T. (1834). *A History of Egyptian Mummies* London: Longman, Rees, Orme, Brown, Green & Longman

Puckle, B.S. (1926). *Funeral Customs. Their Origin and Development* London: T.Werner Laurie

Quigley, C (1998). *Modern Mummies: The Preservation of the Human Body in the Twentieth Century* Jefferson NC: McFarland

Taylor, L. (1983). *Mourning Dress. A Costume and Social History* London: Allen & Unwin

Trompette, P & Lemonnier, M (2007). *The standardization of the supply chain from death to disposal. Interprofessional coordination in the area of care of the dead* ESF Exploratory Workshop paper, Paris

Wilson, J.H. (2011). *The History of Alkaline Hydrolysis* Paper by CEO of Bio Response Solutions, Pittsboro IA

Zbarsky, I. (1997). *Lenin's Embalmers* London: Harvill

Periodicals & other publications

Art Antiquity and Law Volume 1 Issue 4 Dec 1996, pp 414-416, Palmer, N: The Body as Property

The Embalmer Volume 17 No. 2 March 1974

Funeral Director Monitor

Funeral Service Insider Industry News Oct 20 2010: 'America's Veterinarians Helping Families Deal With Pet Loss

Medical Law Review 2007 Herring & Chau: My Body, your body, our bodies

Ibid, 2008 Hardcastle, R: Law and the Human Body: Property Rights, Ownership and Control. Publication review by Gibbons, S.

Mortuary Management Magazine

Oxford Journal of Legal Studies 2008, McGuinness & Brazier: Respecting the living means respecting the dead too

Queensland Parliament Environment and Resources Committee Issues Paper No.3, June 2011: The environmental impacts of conventional burials and cremations

Today's Chemist at Work. Dec 2002, American Chemical Society, pp 33-34, Chemistry Chronicles, McKone, H.T.: Embalming: A "Living" Rite

About the Author

Robert Connolly was born in Liverpool and lived in Australia as a child. He is an artist by training and a graduate of the Royal College of Art and has worked in the art world, mainly as a curator and organiser of exhibitions for the past 30 years; excepting interludes as a civil servant (eating lunch at the same table as serial murderer Dennis Nilsen), working for an American construction company building Canary Wharf in London, and of course, in the funeral industry.

As a performance artist (think Marina Abramovic, Gilbert & George) he beat Lady Gaga to it by 31 years by wearing a suit made of meat at the Slade School of Art postgraduate private view in 1979: http://edible-guest.blogspot.co.uk

He currently runs an arts charity that provides studio space for artists in London, and divides his time between there and Oslo.

"Death is the privilege of human nature, and life without it were not worth the taking."
　　—Nicholas Rowe, 1674 – 1718

Printed in Great Britain
by Amazon